Keltie Colleen

the
dead**x**stop
publishing
company.

The Deadxstop Publishing Company

Chicago

First Edition

DeadXStop.com

KeltieColleenDance.com

For My Army

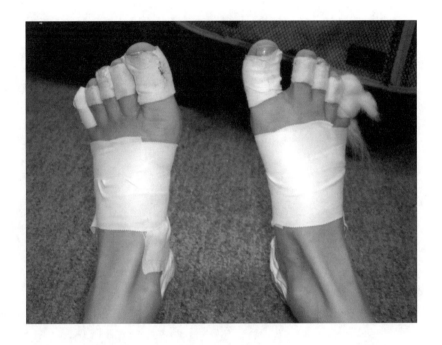

"The bad thing about falling to pieces is that it hurts. The good thing about it is that once you're lying there in shards you've got nothing left to protect, and so you have no reason not to be honest."

— *David James Duncan*

FOREWORD

I can't give you an exact date or tell you what dance studio I was in when I first saw Keltie Colleen. You see, I'm terrible at remembering dates, times and places. I'm ashamed to say it also takes me a while to get names.

What I remember is a person's presence, and I couldn't forget Keltie's. Events and people stick with me based on my emotional response when something special occurs, something magical. My feelings at those moments translate into a stamp – a stamp in time and a moment burned into my mind.

And on that otherwise unmemorable day in an unmemorable studio, I met some of the most talented, beautiful and exciting female dancers I've ever met. In that audition, Keltie stood out. It was her presence! That's what I remember when I audition dancers, singers and actors. Their presence, their sass, their moxie... they're IT! Besides digging her body, her moves, her smile and her craft, I was most impressed with her sense of self, her fun and her confidence. Keltie made a lasting impression at the first dance audition for *Peepshow*. I thought about how I would love to spend eight hours every day in a rehearsal room with that energy.

It would be a few years from that first workshop until the actual first day of rehearsal for *Peepshow*. I was thrilled when Keltie accepted a role in the show. But when I saw her again, something changed. I suspected it was personal, but I didn't want to get into the personal lives of my dancers too soon. So much was at stake in our short window to rehearse. Keltie became thin, too thin. I love all shapes and sizes, but not only was she thin, she was fading. She wasn't present. That glowing presence I fell in love with was half-lit. Faded. Something was up, and not to give anything you are about to read away, let's just say she hit the pavement. Literally!

A few years prior to *Peepshow,* I was asked to direct and choreograph *Legally Blonde: The Musical* on Broadway. I immediately responded "Yes!" I choreographed on Broadway for a few years. I had the pleasure of working on three film-to-stage musical adaptations: *Hairspray, Dirty Rotten Scoundrels* and *The Full Monty.* I collaborated with some of the best directors in the business – Jerome Robbins, Michael Bennett and Jack O'Brien, to name a few. I was ready to take the next step from choreographer to director/choreographer and *Legally Blonde* was a great fit. Plus, I lived the story of Elle Woods. I knew it firsthand, as I too had been dumped.

I'm no psychology major, but I would guess there are two common things that happen to everyone who gets dumped. You cry and say "poor me," and then you pick yourself up, dust yourself off and start all over again after hours of therapy and lots of out-of-pocket expenses!

This is the part I love though! The reinvention. Because somewhere along the way, like Elle Woods, Keltie and I, you lose sight of yourself in relationships. We lost sight of us. And then we had to find us all over again. Who were we? Where did we go? What did we stand for? How did we define ourselves?

When speaking with the brilliant writers of *Legally Blonde: The Musical,* Heather Hach Hearne, Larry O'Keefe and Nell Benjamin, I asked them to come up with a song to help others understand that even after an unthinkable break-up, the road back to yourself can be a positive journey. Not easy, but positive.

Besides, Elle Woods wouldn't have it any other way.

In the last scene, Elle Woods sings to Warner Huntington. He's her boyfriend who broke up with her in the beginning, then proposes to her at the end after he sees her become more successful than he ever imagined her being.

Though I dreamed of this day long ago.
Now my answer is thank you, but no
Look, I've barely begun, I'm hardly through
I was living in ignorant bliss
'Til I learned I could be more than this (Pointing to her blonde hair)
And you know, in a way, I owe it all to you.
I thought losing your love was a blow I could never withstand
Look how far I have come without anyone holding my hand
I had to find my way
The day you broke my heart
You handed me the chance to make a brand new start
You helped me find my way
There's still so much to learn
So many dreams to earn
But even if I crash and burn 10 times a day
I think I'm here to stay
I'm gonna find my way

The truth is, standing on your own will always make standing together in love or work so much richer, and your presence will always be felt.

What happens to any of us in the face of loss, how we respond and rebuild, speaks volumes about who we are and how present we choose to be in life.

Ultimately, love is the one thing we all want and need.

How we choose to find it is another story. I was young and fell head over heels in love. Like Elle and Keltie, when that ended abruptly, I fell apart. Keltie, like so many of us, lost herself in the search for love. But you will see, she also found a much greater self in the trip back to who she is and what she is made of.

It's the one story we want to hear again and again, a love story with a happy ending. Well, this book is one. The love in the end may be self-love when all is said and done, but if you can't find a way to love yourself, how can you ever expect anyone else to?

— *Jerry Mitchell*

Rockettes, Rockstars and Rockbottom

INTRODUCTION

I'm your average, everyday sort of girl. I have mousy brown hair that I color head-turning blonde. I'm too tall to be considered short, but too short to be considered a supermodel. I'm OK at most things. I can cook pancakes and eggs, but you wouldn't want me to make you dinner. I can sing a little. Inside the shower, I sound pretty good… I think. I have a slightly large forehead, an awkwardly pointed nose and suffer from bouts of annoying adult acne. Mixing this together with a pair of perfectly arched eyebrows, a genuine smile of straight pearly whites and golden brown eyes, you get a girl who turns heads when dressed up, but doesn't receive a second glance when grocery shopping at 9 a.m. in sweatpants.

My parents are average people too: a teacher and a mechanic. They've been married an above average 35 years. The average-sized town I was born and raised in has the quintessential number of gas stations and one Wal-Mart.

Ever since I can remember, I wanted to be a dancer. I became hooked on '80s music videos featuring pop starlets surrounded by dancers with perfect hair, trendy costumes and fresh moves. I wanted to live in the world of lighting, camera angles and exotic locations. I wanted to be best friends with the cartoon cat in Paula Abdul's "Opposites Attract" video and was ready to enlist in Janet Jackson's "Rhythm Nation" army. I wanted to be the star behind the star in tap shoes, a leather skirt or a pair of hot pink leggings.

I grew up performing dance moves around my parents' middle-class Canadian home to anyone who would watch. Usually no one wanted to, but I still spent hours in the basement, my feet raw from the burn of twirling and spinning on the brown shag carpet. I watched my reflection from my dad's giant framed Beatles posters. John, Paul, George and Ringo were my only audience, which started my obsession with hippie culture, Ringo Starr and my own reflection. I drained packages of batteries dancing to my bright pink boom box. I owned four cassette tapes: Paula Abdul, Tiffany, Culture Club and Janet Jackson. When I wasn't dancing, I played Monopoly by myself in the corner, being both the thimble and the horse when my brother, three years older, immersed in his quest to reach the next highest score in Super Mario Bros.

I blame growing up in Canada for my politeness. I come from the land of "please" and "thank you." I've never littered so much as a plastic straw wrapper. I don't believe in violence, and feel sick when I watch movies with fight scenes or guns. I walked 30 minutes to school each day in sub-zero winters, sometimes wearing shorts and combat boots. I thought I looked cool, but in retrospect, I was just a teenage idiot. I like nature and animals. If need be, I can build an outdoor emergency lean-to tent out of twigs and a tarp because in eighth grade, I took an Outdoor Education elective. I learned basic first aid, how to build a fire and what deer poop looked like. I received a 98 percent on my report card, which made up for failing French. *Ça va? Say what?* I spent most of Mr. O' Handly's French class staring out the window across the hall where two cute blonde boys from my grade wore Green Day t-shirts and stared back with their impossibly confusing teenage eyes. I could identify deer poop but I couldn't fluently speak one of the two official languages of my country. So very average of me.

At 4 years old, I attended my first Creative Movement class. I banged away on a lime green plastic Fisher-Price drum, but someone whisked me away while the group danced in a circle. Too politely Canadian to interrupt the teacher and ask to use the bathroom, I soaked my pink leotard and tights with bright yellow urine. From a young age, I was unable to ask for what I needed and much too polite for my own good. My life of public embarrassment began.

Years later, I made almost no progress. I was the only dancer who received the honorable mention ribbon at Showstopper, one of the nation's biggest dance competitions. Convinced I was special, I proudly displayed my ribbon during show and tell at school. I later realized honorable mention ribbons were only given to competitors with scores so low, the judges couldn't award an actual medal. At 9 years old, I was terrible and believed I had found my calling.

In high school, I invited my first boyfriend to watch me perform in a showcase at our local theater. Halfway through my routine, a snap on my costume came undone. My red velvet

halter top unitard fell to my hips and I flashed him and most of
my town. At 18 years old, I already crashed and burned so many
times, it didn't faze me. Within the confines of my high school
years, I gulped a cup of the hockey team's urine, and started my
period all over white pants during a class presentation. Losing my
top was just another moment in my embarrassing life. I simply
continued my steps, reached down, pulled up my top and
refastened it. The audience cheered at my resilience. It's not
about what falls on your plate, but what you do with it.
Challenges are about reactions and everyone is waiting to see
yours.

I spent most of my youth being loud and weird in public, but
sullen and introspective while alone in my room at night. I
emphatically scribbled lyrics from my favorite Nirvana and
Smashing Pumpkins songs and plastered them around my
bedroom. My walls were a contradiction, much like myself: a
layer of dark, angsty words surrounded by ballerinas in gorgeous
tutus and tiaras contorted in perfect arabesques.

Idolizing the ballerinas on my wall, I knew dancing was my
destiny. Every evening after my parents kissed me goodnight, I
snuck out from under my covers and quietly did a full workout of
sit-ups, push-ups and stretches. I crawled back into bed, sweaty
and hopeful for the day I could dance on that big stage. I
practiced awards show acceptance speeches nightly and shortly
after, fell into a deep sleep filled with magical dance dreams.

Nothing in my life pointed to a career in entertainment. I
have scrawny, long limbs and when my hair is pulled back in a
bun, the only thing people notice is my five-inch forehead. I
don't come from a "showbiz" family. My uncle isn't a producer at
some multi-million dollar motion picture studio, like most
children in Hollywood these days. My feet are terrible by dancer

standards, my en pointe being unremarkable at best, and I couldn't do the splits until I was 17 years old. Whatever setbacks I encountered, I never gave up. I was a great dancer if you only watched my face. I hoped my body and technique would catch up.

Dancing made me special. When the awkwardness of adolescence caught up with me, I rarely dealt with the cruel punishment from the "cool" kids because I was always at dance class. Dance allowed me to escape from the real life I was so terrible at living. I existed in a dream world of glitter and costumes, of props and pride. I felt happiest alone in my room at night, choreographing entire shows I dreamt of performing for my class. In my dream world, everyone who ever doubted me became a believer.

I knew in my heart that New York City was the only place I would ever be able to make it. After all, they say if you can make it there, you can make it anywhere. I told my parents about my plans to move to the Big Apple and they were thrilled. As usual, they became my supportive cheer team. My mom created lists of things I would need and my dad showed me how to defend myself with a house key between my fingers. Many of my dance peers headed off into the vast world of creating their dream careers, so when it was my turn, my dance studio didn't hold an ice cream cake farewell party or any circus of tearful goodbyes. The move felt more like a mission. Honestly, I don't think anyone in my hometown dance community even thought I would accomplish anything notable, and most likely didn't even realize I was leaving. I never had trouble overcoming fear in life. I guess that's where I got lucky. When I decide to do something, I somehow manage to keep all my fears and insecurities at bay. New York City was where I needed to be, and after telling everyone of my plans, I started packing my bags.

Things in life seem scary and beyond our grasp because that's what society trained us to feel. We're somehow OK with feeling small. I feel the exact opposite. Who are we to *not* follow, chase and hunt down our best in life? I had no idea if I would be successful in New York or if it would eat me up and spit me out within the first few weeks, but I couldn't sit in my hometown wishing I took the chance. I had to just do it and see what would happen. I traveled to New York City once before. I saw Times Square at night, was mesmerized by the giant billboards for Broadway shows, smelled the roasting nuts on the street corner, saw the pigeons flying around on garbage night and experienced being in the back row of a prestigious dance class. The small taste was enough to convince me to move. Sometimes destiny doesn't just plop dreams into your lap, sometimes destiny is the courage to chase after those dreams. I packed Tupperware containers with supplies, bought a $140 bus ticket and a week later, my dad drove me to a Greyhound terminal and helped load my stuff on a bus. Suddenly, he became the worldliest human alive. He rarely gave me advice, but in the moments before I got onboard, he spat out hundreds of cautions. "Peanut, never put your money all in one place. Peanut, don't talk to strangers. Call me anytime and I'll drive to come get you." As the bus drove away, I watched my dad tear up and shove his hands into the pockets of his leather jacket. He watched his baby girl leave home and I watched my small town turn to dust behind the bus. I was completely in awe of my own courage. I was completely unsure of the future. I was never happier.

After two and a half days straight on the bus, I finally reached New York City's Port Authority on 42nd Street. I barely slept, barely ate and was almost robbed in the middle of the night, but I arrived happily and fresh-faced, with nothing to my name except a dance bag full of big dreams. I planned to fight my way into the world of entertainment the only way I knew how: kicking, screaming and often embarrassingly stumbling. I threw myself into womanhood and love in the same way: fearlessly, wildly, with all of my heart and almost none of my brain.

I moved into a housing situation typical for any struggling dancer in New York – a crash pad in Queens shared with four others, who worked as flight attendants. I rented my small room for $500 a month. Included in this amazing price were three sets of stairs between the kitchen and my room, a 20-minute walk to the E train and a family of mice that fed off my pantry items daily. I didn't have the heart to kill them, so my landlord came over twice a week and released them into the street. They always found their way back, and soon, I gave up. After all, the little guys were just trying to get by, and so was I.

A normal day meant waking up early to be first in line for 10 a.m. Broadway auditions I was completely wrong for. Of the 200 girls in line, 95 percent already had a coveted Actors' Equity union card and were called in first to audition. The rest of us stood by, hoping the directors wanted to see our pathetic, non-equity, bottom-of-the-barrel selves after auditioning Broadway's elite for five hours. Most of the time I waited for hours, only to head home without ever putting my dancing shoes on.

The Broadway universe is a Catch-22. You can't get cast in a Broadway show without an Equity card, and you can't get an Equity card unless you're in a Broadway show. I once auditioned for *Man of La Mancha*. Even without the Equity card, I realized I missed something far more important – any trace of Spanish descent. There wasn't a spot in the show for a skinny, blonde, all-Canadian girl. The man selling water on the corner of 38th and 8th outside Ripley-Grier Studios probably knew more about typecasting than I did.

I was constantly confused about where I belonged in the dance world, and was also in a constant state of being lost in New York City. For an entire year, I hopped off the train at Penn Station and walked 23 blocks, from 34th Street to Broadway Dance Center on 57th. A subway stopped just steps away on 49th Street, but I could never figure out how to do it. I got on a train thinking it was the right one, but then ended up somewhere in Brooklyn. Someone finally explained to me that uptown meant trains "went where the numbers went up, so north," and downtown was south, so I started getting a little braver. Maybe I was stupid, but in a sea with rushing waves of people, closing doors and loud noises, it's easy to get lost in the maze of Manhattan.

On a good day, when I could navigate correctly and be allowed to audition, I danced all day and advanced to the final five girls, but was inevitably cut. Disappointed and exhausted, I dragged my heavy dance bag and heavy heart back to Queens. I hated it. And loved it. Because sometimes, the bad parts are sort of the most beautiful. I like a little struggle. I like some blood, sweat and tears. An energy charged through me and I felt alive by dying a little inside.

I worked nights to make rent money. Sometimes I go-go danced at clubs or entertained at Bar Mitzvahs. Sometimes I painted my whole body gold and stood as a human statue at some rich New Yorker's outrageous birthday party. I was a hustler, relentless and determined to do only "dance-related" work and not wait tables. Whatever happened, I didn't want to be a girl who went through life as a something/waitress. If I wasn't booking the best dance jobs, I could "Cha Cha Slide" my way to make rent. Technically, it was still dancing. If I told my parents I started waiting tables, they would question my choice to skip college and move to New York. I enrolled in the school of hard knocks and was determined to be valedictorian.

Little victories always kept me going. The smallest breaks were huge steps. I booked my first commercial dancing for the Spanish lotto. I wore a green wig with eight other girls, and danced to a song I couldn't understand the words to. *Success!*

I stood in the front line at a master contemporary teacher's lyrical class at Broadway Dance Center. She instructed me to demonstrate the warm-up, which is an honor in the dance world. I was the girl in class who everyone wanted to be. *Success!*

Then, I appeared in an infomercial for an acne skin care line. Instead of cash, the company paid me in product. I somehow saw this as a compliment and not an insult about my ever-present acne. I took a million dance classes. Sometimes I stood in the front, confident in my skills, and other times I hid in the back, contemplating ways to slip out unnoticed so I didn't embarrass myself in front of the other dancers.

When I walked to class on 57th Street, I would peer down 5th Avenue and gaze at the beautiful Radio City Marquee staring back at me. Art deco in design, the silver structure famously sticks its fabulousness into the street. The history behind Radio City Music Hall is epic. Built in the 1930s by the Rockefellers, it's an iconic structure housing not only some of the most noteworthy events of the century, but also the Radio City Rockettes. The Rockettes are the most famous dance company in the world, with a legacy spanning more than 75 years. Starting in Missouri in the 1920s, the group moved to Radio City shortly after. They performed in between movie showings, and every Christmas season, star in their own show, the Radio City Christmas Spectacular. The Rockettes are the most beautiful and talented precision dancers in the world and even non-dancers know their famous "eye high kicks." I compared the Rockettes to landing on the moon. It's possible, but I was almost certain I would never do it in my lifetime. I saw nothing in myself that Radio City's posters advertised. I wasn't glamorous, beautiful or perfect. Women like this existed, but I wasn't one of them.

But a few months later, I gathered all of my courage and headed out to Radio City for a Rockettes open call audition. I read about it in a dance trade paper and packed my tap shoes, favorite bodysuit and red lipstick, hoping I was completely wrong about myself. I thought I arrived early, but when I walked on the familiar street, I felt overwhelmed. The line of Rockette hopefuls wrapped around the entire city block on 51st Street, twice. More than 700 tall, beautiful, red-lipped beauties nervously waited, with headshots in hand, for their chance to impress. My stomach twisted and I wanted to run the other way, but I managed to patiently wait in line and eventually approach the large rehearsal hall inside the church of dance, Radio City Music Hall. In groups of 100, women were measured, prodded at and lined up. I somehow managed to take my underconfident eyes off the group and look around, awestruck. Iconic photographs of the world's most famous dancers surrounded me. The next hour was a blur of jazz and tap. Then, I got cut.

Girls everywhere cried and complained in their disdain for being cut. I smiled. I wasn't disappointed, but mesmerized to even set foot inside such a special place. I wanted to absorb the walls and dissolve in the carpet. Lingering back, I wondered how long I could stare before someone kicked me out. Eventually, someone did, but after that day, being a Rockette was my destiny. I tasted the words "Rockette" during meals, I dreamed time-steps when I slept. Another open call was scheduled in a few months, and this time, I would be ready. I started an intense training regime of tap classes, workouts and research. I ordered a custom yellow leotard so I would stand out. I started telling people, "I am going to be a Radio City Rockette."

A few months later, I returned to Radio City for the next audition and danced for my life. I shuffled and kicked with every ounce of courage I had. I was the best version of my dancer self I could be. I traveled home a few weeks later to visit my family, and Radio City Entertainment called while I sat in my childhood bedroom. My mom and I cried tears of joy when they invited me to be a part of the famous Rockette line. I did it. Little itty-bitty Keltie, with the mediocre talent and relentless dedication, was now a world-famous Rockette. I went into the basement and spun around, silently thanking The Beatles for watching me dream all those years.

That Christmas, I learned how to be a Rockette. I cried the first time I walked onstage in my "Parade of the Wooden Soldiers" costume. I worked so hard, I lost 10 pounds. I gained 10 blisters (one on each toe), 20 new best friends and a list of 130 new things totally wrong about the way I danced. The show's directors always seemed to yell a correction in my direction, but I was never happier. My contract lasted 10 spectacular weeks and when it was over, I went back to Queens.

I quickly jumped back into the world of auditions and rejections. I took tons of dance classes. I carried my Radio City Rockette bag like an Oscar around the city. I always made sure the logo faced outward, so whatever unsuspecting New Yorker I ran into would see I was a Rockette. I mattered. I was a city celebrity. Or so I thought.

With my new super credit on my résumé, getting into auditions and booking work became easier. I noticed the look of admiration when a director or producer saw I was a Rockette.

Just a few weeks later when I auditioned for my next big job during the Rockettes offseason, I was thrilled to be hired on the spot. I was ready for the next step. I went back out on tour with a totally different type of show, and fell deeply in love with my very first rockstar.

PART ONE: THE ROCKER

Chapter 1

My first sweet taste of rock 'n' roll happened in Philadelphia – home of the cheesesteak, the Liberty Bell and Rocky Balboa. How fitting that my introduction to the knock-down, drag-out world of rockstars and romance happened in the hometown of the most famous boxer in movie history. How many *Rocky* movies were there? Five? I hope my story of broken and beaten hearts stays a trilogy, but I can't be sure.

Some women look for money in their mates, others look for personality. Me? I look for a guitar strapped to their back and a pair of skinny jeans on their legs.

I met Rocker while working as a touring dancer earning $600 per week as the pre-show act for a headlining rock band on their U.S. club tour. I drove across America with six others and our costumes in a white, nine-passenger van. Each day, we woke up, drove for hours and finally arrived at the next venue. Sleeping stretched out on the van's floor while it bounced down the highway actually became comfortable. When we finally arrived, we crammed ourselves into a tiny dressing room to prepare for the show: curling our hair, throwing on false eyelashes and covering our faces with pounds of glitter. I resembled a 1986 Las Vegas showgirl, complete with fishnets and feathers. I didn't find myself remotely attractive and doubted anyone in the audience would either.

I rummaged around the TLA's backstage area for a place to get ready when I first spotted Rocker. I overheard him ask his friends whether he should braid wooden beads into his four-inch, red sideburns. I pretended to focus on my curling iron and over-colored blonde strands, but I was mesmerized. Did he actually prefer his sideburns that way? Was it so long since his last shower and shave that he didn't notice the two ferret-like animals sleeping on his face? While I contemplated my questions, his ferret infestation became appealing. I stood silently, taking it all in. Rocker smoked, wore a skullcap and smelled like he hadn't showered for weeks. Love at first sight, obviously.

If I had any brains or an ounce of control over my heart, what should've happened next was an "Oh, hell no," then a push-turn, pas de bourrée of feathers and fishnets out the door. Instead, this happened:

"Oh hey, how are you?" Rocker asked.

I planned our wedding. I pictured our children. Years of birthday presents floated in my mind. *Please kiss me. Right now.* My mind raced. I want to know what his skin feels like. I can't form sentences, but if I could, I'd quote something brilliant from Poe. I'd report a fascinating story I read in the newspaper this morning. I'd tell the story of giving my shoes to a child on the side of the road in Honduras. I'd be more than the giggling girl who trips over her own feet. I wish I could wear my layers like sweaters and slowly peel them off. It'll prove I'm more than a typical girl. I wish I were a mind reader. I wish I knew his thoughts, unless of course, he's thinking about something other than kissing me, because in that case, I don't want to know. The way he stands there turns me into an adolescent. Hearing his voice leaves me squeamish. I picked my manicure selection out of hundreds of choices based on what might be his favorite, but I already bit off all my nails in anticipation of seeing him. I'm hanging on the tip of every word he says, but he barely knows I'm alive. Worse, he knows I'm alive and doesn't care. Or worse yet, he knows I'm alive, and thinks I'm a squeamish, obsessive, giggling, strange girl who is just plain weird instead of the überhot, smart, cultured, dream girl I try so hard to act like. *Please, don't just stand there. Kiss me or my heart might stop.*

"I'm good," I replied.

If good girls are attracted to bad boys, then I dealt a game of cards between Tommy Lee, Kid Rock and Steven Tyler. Like Sandy Olsson meeting Danny Zuko, he was leather and I was lace. Or more appropriately, I was white feathers and he, newly beaded facial hair.

The show began and I danced in my cheesy "Viva Las Vegas" outfit, complete with thigh-high, black patent boots. I never measured the heels, but they were so high, I couldn't completely straighten my legs while wearing them, let alone navigate around the amps, wires and beer bottles littering the stage. And by "stage," I mean 10x10 wooden riser in the corner of a smoky, crowded bar. People stood so close, they could reach out and grab us, and most nights, they did. My feet stuck to the spilled beer covering the floor, and I nearly tripped over the discarded bottles. Often, the audience ignored our efforts and chanted the band's name instead of watching us. We couldn't get off stage because the marketing team of some corporate sponsor thought it was a good idea for dancers to open a rock 'n' roll show. It was a stupid idea. It was a stupid costume. I hated the white van. But I loved the money and free MAC make-up. It was my first backstage pass and my first taste of the glamorous world of rock 'n' roll.

Rocker's show was far less cheesy and he didn't mind the beer bottles on stage. Most of them probably belonged to him. He covered the top of his sideburns with a bandana and raced around the stage while playing some of the most amazing, ear-shattering music I ever heard. His fingers moved so quickly on his guitar strings, I felt dizzy. I was in awe of how tight his pants were.

This was rock 'n' roll. I was hooked.

After an hour of brain-pummeling, head-quaking music, I meandered into the cramped backstage area. Proving myself to be the most naïve girl on the planet, I walked by Rocker's dressing room, hoping to catch a final glance of the gorgeous creature in the tight pants. His overweight baboon of a bodyguard greeted me. He looked like he hadn't seen the sun in 25 years and instead sat in a pressure cooker, smoking cigarettes and throwing back Jägerbombs.

"You looking for him?" he asked.

How did he know I was looking for Rocker? He must've read my mind. I realized much later, of course, it wasn't a coincidence. Everyone was always looking for Rocker. Rocker was looking right back.

I learned a few key facts about Rocker. He liked to drink Scotch straight up. Not on the rocks or chilled, just a full glass of Scotch. I'm not sure I ever actually saw Rocker sober during our whirlwind showmance, but at the time, it didn't matter. He smelled like sweat and tasted like alcohol and hint of something else, which I later learned was cocaine. I'm the kind of girl who won't eat eggs if they aren't organic, let alone snort a chemical up my nose. In retrospect, all the signs were there. Rocker stayed up all night, was skinnier than me and was always sweaty. I honestly thought I just made him nervous. I was pathetically naïve.

After swapping phone numbers, we planned a "date" for the next night. We met at a local restaurant and he only ordered Scotch. I ate a veggie burger and fries, mentally debating if it was OK to date someone with slimmer thighs than me. This date wasn't my last encounter with skinny rock 'n' roll legs.

Guitar gods must be bred on some alien planet that pumps musician DNA full of hotness. They're beamed down to earth with tight jeans stuck to their legs, a tattoo on their arms and labeled "rockstars." They're put directly in front of me, and I become infatuated.

About seven minutes into our first date, Rocker kissed me. Maybe he was hungry and decided to snack on particles of food behind my molars. We were all over each other in the middle of the restaurant, but no one cared. I became trickle-down drunk from the whisky on his tongue and got a bit too close for comfort with those ferret-like sideburns on his cheeks.

This was miles away from the ballet school honor roll life I grew up with. Being with Rocker, even for a few moments each night, woke up my soul. For the first time, I was the coolest girl I knew. I was the girl who the boy everyone wanted, wanted. Rocker and I were opposites, except for being perfectionists in our work. Our conversations revolved around how we could improve and further our careers. We were marathon runners of life, only making pit stops for water and lust.

Before I met Rocker, I believed the same rules governed all people. Wrong. Rocker wasn't required to do anything for himself. Living on a tour bus was similar to being a guest on a Royal Caribbean cruise. He was woken up around 1:00 p.m. by someone who was awake since 6:30 a.m. and already loaded his 16 guitars and props into a freezing venue in the middle of some random state. Rocker would groan from a lack of sleep and complain he was hung over. Normal people were on lunch breaks, having already dropped their children off at school and attended four meetings and a conference call long before my glamorous Rocker was summoned to work.

Rocker never wore underwear, which he blamed on a lack of clean laundry on tour. A more accurate explanation is because it's one less thing to peel off when climbing into his 2x6 coffin of a bunk bed at night. Rocker didn't cook or know how to prepare a healthy meal. He started his day by finding the two doors marked "Dressing Rooms" and "Catering." Catering was the place where a crew of men in black cargo pants sat around, drank coffee and complained about catering. It was also the place where Rocker decided he didn't want any of the menu choices and retreated to the bus to pour a Scotch for lunch.

Rocker didn't shower every day. Once a week, the tour bus rolled into an unsuspecting Motel 6, and everyone took turns showering in one room. He always looked dirty because he was.

When was the last time you saw the lead singer of your favorite band wear a watch? Think hard. Can you picture it? Probably not. Rockstars aren't required to know how to tell time. Someone always told Rocker where he needed to be and when he needed to be there. Being on time didn't matter anyway. Rocker always arrived 20 minutes late and without underwear on. I didn't mind the lack of underwear, but the tardiness drove my obsessive-compulsive internal clock crazy.

Despite our differences, or maybe because of them, I was infatuated. My honor student brain exploded after watching him onstage. He was the most gorgeous man I ever set eyes on. Rocker channeled the greats as his hair whipped around and his fingers moved in flashes. His perfect face was the reason why good little girls weren't supposed to listen to rock 'n' roll, and the reason mothers were afraid of Elvis.

Off stage, Rocker acted goofy, fun and was everyone's favorite person. Everyone loved him: tour managers, record label executives, stylists, photographers, reporters, venue managers, caterers, other bands he toured with and even the cleaning staff. It was impossible for me not to love him too. He was the rock 'n' roll prom king. After our first date, we were instantly obsessed with each other. I dove into my relationship with Rocker headfirst and completely fearless. I was his girl, he was my guy and everyone accepted it as fact. Sometimes I would stare at Rocker and wouldn't be able to take my eyes off his face. He was perfect – his lips, his eyes, his talent. And he was all mine.

As we entered another venue a few days later, he grabbed my hand and dragged me into the middle of an empty dance floor in an adjacent restaurant. He spun me around and we danced for two songs, oblivious to anyone watching. Beyond his guitar talents, Rocker was an excellent dancer. He busted out Jackson Five moves, proving he could've easily succeeded as the frontman for a boy band, though the hair, tattoos and sideburns may not appeal to teenage girls the way it appealed to me.

Another night, we ate at a cheesy chain restaurant, the kind with random artifacts placed around the room. Rocker stole a leather whip off the wall and I left with a cowboy hat on my head. In the parking lot, Rocker cracked the whip into the sky, singing at the top of his lungs, admiring me with eyes full of happiness, adoration and understanding. I found my equally crazy, equally carefree partner in life. I searched for someone to run wild with and here he was. Billions of people live on the planet, but in the moments we spent together, my heart was sure nothing else existed.

Later, we found ourselves in a tiny, smoke-filled hotel room with his sister and her boyfriend. We sang songs at the top of our lungs and Rocker never let go of my hand. At his carefree suggestion, we put our bathing suits on and spent the night doing cannonballs into the small hotel pool. It was 4 a.m. and the rest of the world slept. I didn't need sleep because I had happiness. I never felt so free.

New York didn't matter. Dancing didn't matter. Calling my parents didn't matter. I existed only for this. Only for him.

I soared. Rocker studied me and constantly asked questions. What did I think of this? How did I feel about that? He hung on every word I said, as if he only subscribed to the religion of Keltie. I was a goddess. He introduced me to people not as his girlfriend, but as the girl he was going to marry. In the morning, Rocker watched me sleep with a plate of breakfast on his lap. Peanut butter toast with bananas, my favorite.

First loves are delicious in a way only firsts can be. Firsts change you. Being with Rocker was riding my bike without training wheels for the first time, the first day of school or the first time I ever set foot on a stage. A magical, mystical combination of elements, matter and energy combusted in my heart, threatening to explode every time I opened my mouth.

Rocker and I played shows each night and drank until the clash of our worlds made sense. One night, the infamous rockstar god Slash came over from a neighboring tour bus to hang out. *Slash!*

Slash had perfect olive skin and was the prettiest man I ever saw. He was the same man my older brother obsessed about when Guns N' Roses came to my small Canadian hometown. My dad gave him two tickets to the show for Christmas and he skipped around the living room, shouting for joy.

Rocker acted like hanging out with a legend was no big deal and introduced me. Slash responded, "You're right, she is the most beautiful girl in the world." I nearly died. All these rockstars were so charming, which was dangerous. There was nothing real about Slash's compliment, but he actually made me feel like the most beautiful girl in the world! I couldn't wait to tell my brother, but mostly I couldn't wait to get drunk, hop on the bus and sloppily kiss my Rocker.

The first night I stepped on Rocker's tour bus, I was assaulted by an aggressive amount of man smell onboard: a mix of dirty socks, greasy hair, stale beer, Old Spice aftershave, rotten bananas, malt liquor and a used gym towel.

The entire kitchen area of the tour bus was filled with bottles of booze and once again, it was easy to understand how Rocker fit into those skinny jeans. I instantly felt fat and vowed to go on a Rocker-inspired liquid diet.

Rocker's small bunk area didn't shock me, but the ratio of alcohol space to people space did. When he first opened the curtain to reveal his tiny sleeping quarters, five full-sized bottles of assorted drinks lined the bunk, covering at least 20 percent of the area. I wondered if alcohol seeped into his skin while he slept by osmosis. Sleeping in a tour bus bunk is like being in the middle of a plastic covered slide at the park. You're surrounded on every side, with only enough room for one sleeping position – on back, legs straight and face six inches from the ceiling.

In the lounge, leather bench seats in a dirty off-white color lined the back area. Most tour buses are set up the same way. Front bench seats rest next to big windows and a television. There's always a small kitchen table attached to the wall with some counter space, a fridge and a sink. Next to that, a bathroom with just a toilet and sink. A curtain or door will lead to the back sleeping section. Three bunks rest on top of each other for three rows back. A fabric curtain covers each bed to offer privacy, but there really isn't any. You can hear everything: movements, snoring, breathing, coughing, talking, sighing… anything. It's like putting a sheet between the person you're sitting next to and hoping you won't hear them. When we were finally lucky enough to be alone, we'd lock the back door to the bunk area, close the shades and flip on some music.

After his set, Rocker's 21-year-old chest dripped with sweat. Tattoos covered almost every part of his body, whether it was small Chinese characters on his neck or a Batman logo across his belly. Some were slightly scary skulls and crossbones or very scary bleeding faces. Ballerina and bleeding faces, we were obviously a perfect match.

I watched 15 minutes of one scary movie in my entire life. If I watched anything scary, awful nightmares kept me awake. Perhaps some higher power was telling me to stay away from this creepily tattooed, sweaty young man, but I closed my eyes and tried to land my equally sweaty body on the dirty back lounge bench, careful to avoid the floor below. The floor was a sticky, smelly mess, covered with spilled drinks. If by chance, we ended up on the floor and were desperate enough for a drink, we could ring out the carpet and fix ourselves a nightcap.

A week later, the tour ended. Rocker and I promised to visit soon. Before the end of the tour, I think Rocker asked me to be his girlfriend and I possibly agreed. I can confirm he made me listen to the entire Abbey Road album because he said it would change my life. I passed out drunk sometime in the middle of "Octopus's Garden." I can't recall anything after. Regardless if I was coherent enough to notice it, my life drastically changed.

Chapter 2

The end of tour meant returning to my hectic life in New York City. Luckily, the same year I moved to New York was the same year my childhood best friend, Spagatti, also moved. Spagatti and I grew up down the street from each other in Canada. Our families were best friends. His sister was in my grade and at one point, he was my tap teacher. We danced together our whole lives and were equally nerdy in totally different ways. For most of my life, Spagatti was my makeshift boyfriend without anything lovey or physical. I didn't need a supportive, smart, caring, emotionally available guy to date because I had Spagatti. And since we were best friends, we never had to deal with a break-up.

Spagatti won quite a few trophies growing up. I did not. I went on quite a few dates growing up. He did not. We spent our teen years bonding over Saturday morning dance classes, Wendy's Frosties and Bon Jovi tunes. I considered him my brother. Spagatti knew me better than anyone and always got the truth out of me. He always saw through my acting abilities and called me out when he knew I was lying. We loved each other like brother and sister. We annoyed each other like brother and sister.

We didn't plan on moving to New York at the same time, but we both ended up working in the dance world there.

Spagatti pursued a different part of the industry and overnight, became best friends with every dancer in New York. Instead of auditioning after class or recounting his flaws on long walks from the subway like me, he networked during delicious meals at the West Side Diner beside Broadway Dance Center. Most of these lunches were with my dance idols and people I tried to get to notice me. The tables had turned from the days when I was the one invited into the elite crowds. I was an outcast and Spagatti was Mr. Congeniality.

Spagatti struggled too though. He lived in Queens and couldn't afford air conditioning. The bugs in his third story walk up were the size of quarters. When we got together, we drank hot tea in the middle of summer. We walked around his neighborhood and ate silver dollar pancakes at local diners. His soft flannel sheets reminded me of my parents' house. I slept over a lot because he was my only family in New York. When I lost myself in the sea of 12 million people, I found my truest self in a conversation with him.

Spagatti hated the idea of me getting involved with Rocker. One night, as we walked back from picking up our Chinese takeout, he said, "This guy is gonna hurt you, Keltie."

I thought he was wrong. He wasn't, of course. He never is.

Chapter 3

After a month of being disheartened with the dance world in
New York City, I went back on the road to spend time with my
junior Mick Jagger, hoping for a little bit of trickle-down Rocker
happiness. Rocker gloated that he owned 13 pairs of Chuck
Taylors. I stopped myself from asking, "What's a 'Chuck Taylor?'"

Clive Davis signed Rocker for millions, and he was set to be
the next big thing in rock 'n' roll. I only had $900 to my name.
Living in New York City was expensive and I hadn't worked in
months. The plane ticket I bought to visit him cost me $600.

I tried to get closer to Rocker. He smoked, so I started
smoking. He wore black clothing, so I wore black clothing. I was
intoxicated by his charm and his Scotch. When he laughed, he
threw his entire body into it, opening his mouth and grinning
widely. I found the tiny space between his two front teeth
adorable. When he smiled at me, I felt like the most important
person in the world. I hung on his every word the same way my
lips hung on his every breath. But soon enough, it was time to
return to New York and be a dancer. He stayed on the road.

Our next fragment of time together was a few weeks later.
We passed the time with texts and late-night phone calls. I always
wanted more. We planned to meet in New Jersey, where his band
opened for Mötley Crüe on their summer tour. Rocker began to

represent everything. From a young age, boys measured my worth. Not in self image, but in the debt I invested in relationships. If had everything I wanted, including a cute boy, then it was in fact everything I wanted. If I had everything I wanted, and the cute boy was missing from the equation, I needed more. I didn't know how to feel great without someone of the opposite sex telling me I was great.

My pad in Queens was always abuzz as my flight attendant roommates came and left from trips all over the world. Every morning, clumps of cute girls pulled rolling suitcases down the street, wearing knee-length skirts and French twists in their hair. It was the middle of summer and I finally became a woman, living the exciting life I always dreamed of, almost. I lived in New York, worked as a dancer and dated a rockstar. But with no money and only a few friends, I could only hope for the future.

Walking home one day from the subway stop in Queens, I started to feel tired. I wanted to close my eyes and take a nap, right at that moment. It was only two o'clock in the afternoon. I threw up in my mouth.

Once the nausea passed, I reminded myself to eat better and drink more water. I was running myself ragged, trying to create this amazing dance career, working all day and staying up all night texting the boy toy of my dreams.

A few days later, I drove down to New Jersey for Rocker's show with his amazing sister, "McCheese." We sung to Jason Mraz in her Mini Cooper. It took hours to get there but when we finally arrived, I ran out of the car and Rocker ran toward me. I jumped into his arms. He let go, playfully poked me in the chest and asked, "Where did these come from?" I wore one of my favorite low-cut, black tanks. I laughed and smiled. My bust was less than a 32A my entire life. Blame it on ballet school or my dancer body, but I've always been a leg woman. Chest men stay far away from me. I looked down and for the first time, realized what I was no longer missing. My chest was swollen, sore and growing. Rocker jokingly said, "I sure hope you're not pregnant," and we both laughed it off.

Mötley Crüe's concert was insane. They are some of the ugliest men, but they put on one heck of a show. Fire, girls, earplugs, girls, dancing, girls, leather pants and more girls. After the show, I met Tommy Lee and he was just as dirty as I expected.

Inside the back lounge of his tour bus, Rocker decided to start tattooing all of us. He recently purchased a tattoo gun and started practicing on his legs. The thing about tattoo artists is this: they are *artists!* You need some artistic ability to tattoo. Rocker could doodle, at best. He was also close to being completely wasted, as was I. His shaky hands could only draw a star, and I agreed to let him tattoo my hipbone with one. I screamed with pain, but still felt cool. Now, I could find a pair of Chuck Taylors and actually be cool in the insane rock 'n' roll world. I could throw out my Gap jeans and sweaters and become a hard, leather-wearing kind of chick. I smoked, drank and was never more untrue to myself. I was in trouble.

A few weeks passed and I was back in my twin bed sleeping through the night. Unfortunately, I was also sleeping through my days. I finally realized I was missing something very important – my period. Worried, I walked to the drugstore on the corner and bought a box of pregnancy tests. At home, I peed on the famous stick and was relieved when I saw it was negative. Maybe all the pheromones floating around my body told my brain to grace me with a bigger rack. I once again promised myself to eat better, drink less, rest and somewhere in the middle of that, dance.

Rocker came to New York City to celebrate McCheese's birthday and I bought us all tickets to see my favorite musical, *Rent*. I was so excited to finally show him something I was passionate about and as usual, he was up for anything. Rocker's excitement for life was unmatched by anyone else. He brightened any room he was in and every second became an unforgettable memory. The morning of McCheese's birthday, my agent called. I was invited to two last minute auditions for big-budget dance jobs. Perfect timing, since the *Rent* tickets cost most of my rent for the next month.

All I wanted to do was stay in bed with Rocker, but I got up. I never give up career options for anyone. I always auditioned and said yes to work. Not even a perfect morning with Rocker could stop that. I pulled on an outfit, grabbed my headshots and resume, and headed into the city. I could meet up with Rocker and his sister later for *Rent*. Until then, I needed to land a job, so I could pay mine.

I arrived on 17th Street for my auditions in a jean skirt and a gray sweater. The address was different, but the protocol was always the same. Push my way through a large, overcrowded hallway to find the sign-in sheet. Sign my name and phone number. Check the box for female. Check the box for Caucasian. Hand in my headshot and resume. Wait anywhere between five minutes and three hours for the production assistant to call my name. Walk inside a small room with a video camera facing a green screen. State my name and contact information. Do whatever zany thing the production assistant asked me to.

I was instructed to jog around the room. After almost 20 years of dance classes, I was showing off my jogging skills? I couldn't remember the last time I jogged. Throughout high school, my mom wrote notes excusing me from physical education classes, so I wouldn't ruin my dance career with a broken leg or dodgeball to the shin. Besides dancing, I was a klutz in every athletic activity. Jogging felt totally unnatural. Jogging in a jean skirt and boots in a 6x8 room on camera was the worst.

Next door, I went through the process again for the second audition. This time, the production assistant ordered me to dance around the room with a shoebox, like a dancing saleswoman. I liked shoes. I wished I could afford to buy more. At least I could semi-relate to this character. Afterward, I rushed uptown to meet Rocker and his sister, glad the auditions were over and sure I wasted my time.

The Nederlander Theatre showed *Rent* like every night, and I gazed onto the stage filled with ladders, trash cans and Christmas lights. Mark sang, "December 24th. 9 p.m. Eastern Standard Time. From here on in, I shoot without a script," and once again my favorite world drew me in. The world where messed up people, starving artists and flamboyant characters chased their dreams in the best city in the world. I always related to the character of Mimi, someone with two different personas: big, bold and fearless and then shy and timid, wanting to find her home in someone's arms. I grabbed Rocker's leg as she and Roger sang, "Light My Candle." He smiled, and I was happy he loved this world as much as I did.

I fell madly in love with Rocker in such a short amount of time, but I couldn't help it. He took my breath away. It was impossible to act cool and unaffected because he completely altered the inner workings of my heart. When he kissed me, balloons and streamers burst out of me, Macy's Thanksgiving Day Parade style. As much as I loved him, my emotions faltered. I couldn't balance the person I pretended to be and the person I actually was. Every breath, every word he spoke became my words to live by. I gave him every part of myself and he didn't even realize.

At intermission, McCheese and I went to the bathroom, and when I opened my purse, the extra pregnancy test I purchased a few days before fell out. A bout of cramps still hadn't visited me, so I decided to pee on it, just so I could tell myself everything was OK. Everything was not OK.

Inside the second stall of the balcony bathrooms at the Nederlander, two lines showed up and my worst fears were confirmed. I was pregnant. I was shocked. I walked out of the stall, looked McCheese in the eyes, and said, "Um, I'm pregnant." She was in shock too. We said nothing else and walked back to our seats just in time for the second act. I shook through Mimi's haunting rendition of "Without You," tears streaming down my face, more scared than ever. I lived my life as a responsible perfectionist, and here I was with an unwanted pregnancy from a boy I knew less than three months, with barely enough money in my pocket to buy groceries.

The rest of the show was a blur. When Angel passed away in the second act and we reached the ever-famous scene, I could barely breathe. I was so careless, and now I was hopeless.

After the show, Rocker decided to make the night more exciting by hailing a bicycle cab. The three of us were peddled down Broadway and through Times Square. In the open summer air, we sang "New York, New York" at the top of our lungs. Rocker laughed his signature laugh, mouth wide open and bright eyes staring at the city. He had no idea his life was about to change.

We walked into one of my favorite rock 'n' roll bars in the city, Snitch. It was dingy and the floors were sticky from spilled beer. The walls were covered with old band posters and stickers.

Rocker ordered us some drinks at the bar, as McCheese and I headed to the bathroom. We wrote our initials across the first bathroom stall where it stayed for years after. I watched some girls in the bathroom snort cocaine off a house key. Rock 'n' roll.

We stood by an open window overlooking 23rd Street. Garbage night in New York City, piles of trash littered the sidewalks.

Rocker walked across the room and handed me a tequila shot. I looked him in the eye and said, "I have something to tell you," and then, "I'm pregnant." He immediately asked, "Are you going to keep it?" I hadn't thought that far ahead. I was still in shock. I certainly couldn't support a child and I didn't think Rocker was ready to be a father. I was scared. I told him what I thought he wanted to hear and answered, "No." He motioned to the glass in my hand. "Well then," he said, "you may as well have that shot."

Two days later, I filmed an international commercial for one of the world's most famous shoe companies. When I arrived for work and saw I had to wear a sports bra, I was terrified. My pregnancy was months away from ever showing, but I felt so breakable. When I walked on set and stepped in front of the giant cameras, I was sure that people could see right through my skin and into the sin growing inside me. I felt like they knew my secret and judged me from behind the lens. But my acting abilities fooled them and I turned on my charm. Truthfully, I was exhausted, sick to my stomach and surprised at my own strength for making it through the 14-hour shoot.

The next day, I called Planned Parenthood. When I told the woman on the line that I was pregnant, the words seemed foreign on my own lips. I felt like an actress in an after school special. Was this my life? She took my name and information casually, as if I called to make an appointment to get my teeth cleaned. After I hung up, I cried for the next seven hours. Alone. I told no one else what happened. Not my parents, not my friends, not even Spagatti.

Planned Parenthood scheduled my appointment for the next week. Rocker was on tour and couldn't, or wouldn't, come with me. Ever since I told him the news of our pregnancy, he changed. It was difficult for my mind to process and seemed almost impossible for his 21-year-old mind to comprehend. He distanced himself from me in every way. He saw me as a tainted, emotional mess who was taking a toll on his easy-going, partying ways. I looked for some real support and received none. I was so lost.

Around the same time, my parents called. They just returned from their first vacation in three years since my brother was involved in a tragic workplace accident that left him unable to walk. He spent his days in between back surgeries in bed with heavy prescriptions, including morphine and antidepressants.

Doctors prescribed a magic soup of pills so he couldn't feel his spine or realize how bad his life was. My handsome, vibrant, popular brother morphed into a bed-ridden patient. His blue eyes didn't sparkle the few instances he awoke from his drug-induced sleep patterns. My parents arranged for people to help my brother while they were away, but didn't realize how sick he became. He was sick to his stomach and vomited out all of his medications. No big deal when it's just cough syrup, but the prescriptions were so intense, his body went through withdrawals and he started experiencing seizures and immense pain. A nurse arrived the next day to find my brother in a pile of his own vomit, still having seizures. He was rushed to the hospital and my parents came home. When they called me, the guilt set in.

Who was I to be a bright shining star? Who was I to move so far away that I couldn't and wouldn't help? Who was I to play rockstar girlfriend with my brother's idols while he lay at home barely coherent? A fog of guilt surrounded me. I avoided my family because when I spoke to them, they reminded me of how awful things were at home. I liked to pretend it didn't exist. But it did, and it hurt my soul. I wanted my relationship with Rocker to be worth something, but the more pressure I put on him, the more he pulled away. I didn't hear from him for days. Our showmance was ending. The heavier my thoughts and words became, the less Rocker wanted to do with them. He wanted a fun party girl. I wanted a boyfriend. I wanted a father for the little seed inside me.

A few days later, my agent reminded me of a second commercial I was booked to dance in. I signed a contract and needed to arrive in Connecticut to shoot on location. Leaving my apartment was the last thing I wanted to do. Working meant getting out of the cocoon of sadness I created in my twin bed. Working meant showering. Working meant stopping the crying. I didn't think I could accomplish one of these things, let alone all of them, but I had to. Calling my parents for money meant admitting the disaster my life became. Just the thought was enough to at least get me into the shower.

I somehow managed to smile my way through work. The choreographer was well-prepared and made my job easy. The not-so easy part was that he and Rocker shared the same name. I spent the six hours of rehearsal shouting his name repeatedly. Where is the arm? Where do you want me to stand? What happened on count five?

Hearing his name hundreds of times reminded me that Rocker was nowhere to be found. He didn't answer the phone.

We hadn't spoken. I wrote in my journal for hours. I tried to map out exactly when things went wrong. What did I do wrong? Falling in love is easy, but falling out is the hardest thing. It's so easy to say, "I fell in love the instant you said my name," but how do you pinpoint the exact time when things went wrong? Was it the shirt I wore? Was it something I said? Did I have bad breath? Did I call too many times? My list of things wrong with me grew exponentially. I never paused to think it might be something to do with him. Love, whether it lasts one day or 10 years, is never easy to lose. Once love lets its feelings loose in your bloodstream, there's no turning back. You breathe differently. You talk differently. You are different.

I walked around the parking lot to clear my head. I expected so much from myself without ever checking in to make sure I could still breathe. I pounded the pavement with all of the hurt in my soul for more than two hours and finally broke down. But I was still alive. I breathed. I watched the clear night, full of stars. Contrary to what it felt like, this was not hell.

After the shoot, I took the bus back from Connecticut and began to feel sick. A fever turned into the shakes, which turned into lightheadedness. When I arrived at Port Authority, our group split up, and a concerned dancer asked if anyone was picking me up. I told her I was taking the subway home. I called Rocker but I couldn't speak and could only cry and shake. The pain was unimaginable, the worst cramps I ever felt in my life. Something was very wrong with me. In the bathroom, I almost collapsed in a stall. I looked in between my legs and found a bloody mess. I was losing the baby.

I was so weak that a friend called a taxi for me. As I loaded myself into the back seat and whispered my address to the driver, I remember wanting to die. I didn't care if I ever made it home because my life was over. Life changed and my innocence was lost. I curled up on the floor of the car and cried. When we finally arrived in Queens, I managed to pay the driver and crawl out of the cab. I was in so much pain that I couldn't stand up, let alone walk. I collapsed on the front stoop of my apartment building and stayed there until my landlord noticed me. He pulled me inside and helped me up the stairs. I told him I had the flu. I lay in bed for three days by myself. I didn't tell anyone else what happened. Rocker knew, but he never came to help me. I couldn't walk, speak or eat. I mourned the loss of something I never even wanted. Loss is like that. It doesn't matter what you're losing, but if you are losing something, you have lost. My life was over.

I spent a week staring at my phone waiting for a call or text. Rocker booked a show in New York City, so I dragged myself out to 34th Street to shop for something "hot" to wear. He didn't even know I was coming. I kept telling myself he was busy, but he was straight up avoiding me. For some reason, I thought being "hot" was the answer. My pain didn't matter as long as I kept an attractive outward appearance. If I walked down the street and construction workers whistled at me, everything would be OK. Though all my pain, I was determined to hold it all inside. To still be cool and play with my rock 'n' roll boy as if nothing happened. My heart was broken. Rock on.

I found a black corset, heels and squeezed into a pair of tight jeans. Rocker and I hadn't spoken in days, but I headed to the show anyway with his sister. From the moment I got out of her car, everything changed. He didn't run to me or hold me. Instead, he barely spoke and found any excuse to stay away from me. The only thing he managed to say was, "I'm sorry." As if everything could be fixed with a simple apology. My heart sank, but I acted cool and drank my blues away. Inside, I crumbled. It was over. Just seven days after I lost our child, I lost Rocker.

Chapter 4

I took the break-up badly. I cried, pleaded and called all of his friends. Rocker was the first person I ever fell in love with. It was a free, careless kind of love where we were the only two people who existed. But now he was gone and I found myself unable to deal with the pain. I hated him and loved him at the same time.

To cope, I took dance classes, wrote and cried. Nothing helped. The next few weeks blurred by and suddenly, I found myself packing my suitcase full of leotards and tights, ready to start my second contract as a Radio City Rockette. This job was a dream of mine for so long, but the summer was so painful, both the rhinestone encrusted costumes and joyful Christmas music were completely lost on me. Surrounded by 20 of my best girlfriends, I still felt alone. I was a walking zombie in tights. People around me talked and I saw them, but I stayed deep in my own head, like someone pressed mute on my world's remote control. The only thing resonating was my own voice yelling, "Come back." I took sleeping pills every night and felt completely numb during my eight-hour rehearsal days. Hundreds of kicks each day and still nothing. My heart was so sore, my brain didn't even acknowledge the pain in my hamstrings.

The Radio City Rockettes take their show seriously. The Christmas Spectacular is an international symbol synonymous with the city of New York for more than 75 years. There are more than 10,000 numbers and depths on the Radio City stage. The center of stage is labeled "0." Every foot, heading both right and left of center, is labeled with another number, all the way out to 34. From front to back, there are an additional 10 lines across the stage, called depths.

Being a Rockette is like playing Battleship, only we position ourselves while turning, kicking and strutting in three-inch heels. Six on the dash. Eighteen on the circle. If I wasn't already sick to my stomach, dancing on the tilt-a-whirl that is the Radio City stage would do it for me. When we line up in preparation for our famous kick-line, there is actually a difference between having the tips of our toes directly behind the line (toeing) and having the arches of our feet splitting the line (arching). The difference seemed silly to me, but it means the world to the Rockettes.

The Rockettes are precise. Dancers are taught where their eyes should be focused on at any given moment. My eyes should've focused on stage right, to the first level of seats. Instead, I saw the world upside down and backwards, in a solid state of confusion, self-loathing and despair. We were worked to the bone. I woke up each morning, dressed myself in black tights and a black leotard and slicked my hair back into a French twist. I went to the rehearsal hall, taped up my feet and did a 45-minute warm-up for my muscles.

We danced for hours and received tough love from dance captains and directors. There's never a point in Rockette season where you can just glide through. I pushed myself, tap dancing and acting my way through the depression, even though my heart and brain were ready to burst. Only a few people noticed my sadness. One night, my friend Becca came into my hotel room and said, "Maybe if you stopped listening to sad music, you'd feel better." I listened to Ryan Adams on repeat for almost a month. I cried every day. I couldn't watch television. I couldn't go to the movies. I was antisocial and drank constantly. White wine was my new boyfriend. He didn't taste as sweet as Rocker.

Rehearsals finished and we opened the Christmas show. Instead of long rehearsal days, I spent my time inside dark theaters performing multiple shows. I arrived at 9 a.m., applied my signature lashes and red lips, and took care of my body. I forced my swollen feet and legs into a pair of suntan tights and used as many pins as I could to secure the oversized, white marabou hat to my head. My scalp was raw, red and agitated, which matched the condition of my heart perfectly. Most days, I thought about poking my eyeballs out with those pins. In break-ups, it's easy to convince yourself that you'll never meet anyone like "them" again. I was totally unaware of the dozens of charming rocker boys dying to break my heart. Rocker wouldn't be the first. I never got better at the break-up part either. I did get better with each Rockette holiday season with my flaps, ball changes and kicks, but in love, it never got less confusing or easier.

I waited in the wings and heard the hush of the audience sweep over the theater as the lights dimmed and the performance started. I succumbed to the blackness, devoid of any happiness. Before my cue, childhood Keltie whispered in my ear. Dancing was my dream. I should be happy. As my tap shoes clinked onto the stage, I transformed into a joyful Roxstar, happily reporting to the wide-eyed audience that they'd better be good because Santa Claus was coming to town. I repeated this process three or four times a day, totaling more than six hours of dancing. I ran a Christmas marathon in three-inch heels, doing my best to hold it together. Exhausted from my happy Christmas act at the end of the show day, I dragged an unsuspecting Rockette to a local dive bar and drank until I stopped hurting, or until I passed out. I was loud and out of control. I met a local, made out with him, stopped and cried to him for hours. I was a complete mess. I was also screwing up my reputation with all the people who mattered most to me. The cast thought I was a party girl and I acted like I didn't have a care in the world. I walked onstage for a 10 a.m. show one Saturday morning still smelling last night's wine on my breath.

I was the queen of bandages. I taped up every inch of my feet before shows. I danced on my disasters of limbs all day, came home, cooked dinner and tried to ignore the white tape covering the feelings I had no desire to deal with. Before bed, I peeled away the bandages until I could see the pain just as much as it stung. I saw myself – infected, gross, dirty, used, callused, torn and beaten.

I was stuck in an unhealthy routine. Each morning, I prepared myself for a good day. When the girls asked me how I was, I'd reply, "Wonderful." I chose not to chat about the negative on the way to work, hiding myself behind a newspaper and tea. I loudly greeted every member of the staff. I smiled and giggled, always finding a way to joke around and make the day brighter for anyone who stood next to me. I tried hard to compliment my friends when they danced brilliantly. At lunch, I told stories. I acted silly. I put my issues in the, "I never really cared" category, covering up that I really did care.

When I came home, I stared at the ceiling and tried to understand my life. How did I allow so many amazing things to turn sour? I concentrated on the perfections of others and only saw the imperfections in myself. I stripped away my layers of protection, just like my bandages, and was left with an open sore. It hurt. It hurt for everything in the world, for the things I never said, and for the things I should've said. It hurt for the ones I let get away and the ones I never allowed to get close to me. It hurt for the person I wanted so badly to become and the exhaustion from daily pep talks. It hurt from pumping life into a body unable to take a break. It hurt for the lies I told Rocker and the lies I accepted from him. It hurt for the way my life turned out, compared to my potential. It hurt from having the power to inspire everyone but myself to live better. I ached for the universe to give me something else. To show me what was next. I couldn't control my restlessness.

At some point after the tipsy 10 a.m. Rockette show and the 57th solo walk on the beach where I cried my eyes out, I decided it was time to take all the tape off. To take a day for myself and lick my wounds instead of covering them up. The easiest solution is never the answer, but I vowed to be a better person. I quit drinking, stayed in my room and read books. During New Year's Eve, I spent the night in bed, staring at the television while one of the bands from Rocker's tour on played on screen. The image stung like a fresh wound.

I compared adulthood to middle school. We all see the movies and read the books or see others go through the motions. But unless we have a chance to live life, we never really know what to do when faced with adversity. We need to make mistakes to learn. We can't expect ourselves to deal with everything the "right way," when we never went through it before. I needed to learn for myself that it was OK to fall off the bike sometimes, and when I was a little stronger, I could get back on.

Rocker was awful to me. Maybe not on purpose, but he left a huge and deep scar. I mistakenly trusted him. When our relationship was over, it was a mistake to hold onto the pain for so long. But the thing about mistakes is, they need to be forgiven.

I would try hard to forgive and let go. Instead of being the queen of bandages, I chose to be the queen of forgiveness.

Buddha taught me, "To forgive is holy." We all screw up. Rocker really screwed up, but for some reason, he was able to go back to his glamorous life, while I was stuck picking up the pieces. It's unfair that the people who make the mess are rarely the ones to clean it up. Those of us left behind have to sweep our hearts off the floor and into the dustpan, trying to figure out how to make them shiny and new again.

I lived on a diet of avocados and nacho chips. My roommates questioned if I had an eating disorder, but I told them I had a broken soul and time was the only cure. I wished someone would commit me to the "heartbreak" ward of the hospital and mend me with hugs, romantic comedies and Jell-O served with tiny plastic spoons.

The New Year came and went, and my contract of kicks, wine and sadness ended. I returned to New York in one shaky, barely together piece and moved back into my mouse-infested apartment in Queens. I was thin. I was tired. I was again, unemployed. One of my favorite, delightfully gay chorus boys from the show moved in with me. Having him around should've helped me build my broken self-esteem, but that was a lost cause. I did start dressing better and buying more fabulous shoes, though.

I walked through dance classes, auditions and life carrying my sadness around in my dance bag, beside my headshots and in between my tap and ballet shoes. But eventually, I felt ready for the next step, even if I was totally unsure what it was.

PART TWO: THE SINGER

Chapter 5

My men always liked to sleep around and musician number two happened to be sleeping with someone I couldn't compete with: Jesus.

I met my second rockstar in the middle of a cold, dry winter in the city. Frozen New York hid under a constant blanket of gloomy clouds, and so did my heart. I wasn't looking for a boyfriend, I just walked down the street, hoping every person I passed considered me the perfect female specimen and fell madly in love with me.

I broke my promise to myself to live better. I still went to dance classes and auditions during the day, but when the evening settled over the city and my friends dated or snuggled up to their lovers, I snuggled up to bottles of wine, alone.

One of the Rockette sisters I stayed close with invited me out in the sub-zero night for music and drinks at a swanky, elite Billboard party in Manhattan. I instantly said yes. Only music could drag me out into the freezing weather. Where there was music, there were musicians. Where there were musicians, there was bound to be skinny jeans. Where there were skinny jeans, there would be a guy wearing said jeans, playing said music, and

if he had a guitar strapped to his back, he would also have a brand
new admirer. Me.

I walked into the Billboard Underground party thinking I
was cooler than cool in my black lace bra and sheer t-shirt. That's
when I saw his fuzzy brown beard, shaggy shoulder length hair
and deep brown eyes. His band epitomized New York City. In any
other city, his short, stocky frame and tattered vintage clothes
would allow anyone to mistake him for a homeless person.
Typical super trendy musician hipster, you can't tell if they
spend enormous amounts of money at Urban Outfitters to look
homeless, or if they really are homeless. He embodied homeless
chic. He wore an army jacket, a vintage t-shirt and a wool scarf
tightly around his neck. Whatever the Lower East Siders of
Manhattan wear one day, it's the fashion sold at Target the next
year. He drank a cup of tea. He wore white Chuck Taylors. I
thought about Rocker and the bright yellow pair he bought
before we fell apart. I pictured him dancing down the street in
his tight jeans and perfect new shoes.

My Rockette sister introduced me to Singer and his group
of friends. I should've bolted out the door, but I admired this
fellow's thoughts and said what I thought he wanted to hear. I
loved everything he loved. I wanted to eat what he wanted to eat.
I wanted to drink the same wine he did. Typical Keltie.

He was a brilliant songwriter. I watched him and his
bandmates play a set for a room of music journalists and other
aficionados. I cried as he sang the final song of the night, a
haunting acoustic ballad. His voice sounded like the inside of my
soul. He was raspy, dark and beautiful. He would be mine. My
heart ached with every word of Singer's folk pop mix. He sang
the soundtrack to my life. His thoughtful voice intoxicated the
crowd and everyone in the room silently stood. There wasn't a

dry eye in the room, including my own.

Some little girl is eyeing me
Throwing me smiles that I can't see
'Cause she's not you.

I thought of Rocker. I missed him. I wanted to replace him. So I did.

A group of us went out for dinner after Singer's show and I turned on my Keltie charm and flirted girlishly. I became quite tipsy after drinking away my nerves. He was cute and my self-esteem was in shambles. Regardless of Singer's personality, the idea of him excited me. It never occurred to me that Singer was uninterested or maybe, he didn't find me charming. Dating someone was equivalent to me deciding that I was going to date them, and then letting them know. I decided Singer would be my boyfriend, so he was.

After I met Singer, some friends told me it seemed like I only invited toxic people into my life. Their actual words were "biohazardous waste." I didn't agree that Singer was toxic. I just get myself into impossible situations, and then I waste energy on making impossible things possible. Dancing is a fiercely physical and mentally demanding career. Instead of putting my energy into relationships, my efforts should've focused on myself and my jacked up body. Everything ached and it was in my best interest to keep my heart locked up so it never ached too. I wish they made anti-inflammatories for the heart. I would've bought them in bulk.

Chapter 6

Singer and I started hanging out and things moved slowly. He sat patiently as I told him my tales of being burned. I kept a collection of war stories inside my heart and an equally messy collection calloused on my feet. I fought against myself on two fronts, in love and in my career. Singer listened attentively and we cautiously showed our scars to each other.

We spent our evenings talking in his tiny studio apartment. He never called me by my full name and instead called me "K.C." I liked his pet name and more, I liked being his pet. He was just as lost as me, and every big break and misstep in my dance career paralleled Singer's experiences as he struggled to make a name for himself in music. We were in a relationship, but really, we were cheerleaders for each other's dreams. We wouldn't let each other give up and I was thankful, because on several days, I thought about lying down in the middle of the street and calling it quits.

Singer's East Village studio apartment had red walls, a pull out bed and no windows. I equated him to Donald Trump for having a place like this to himself in the coolest neighborhood in New York City. A night in his studio apartment was a night at the Four Seasons compared to my apartment in Queens. We frequented a store in the neighborhood called Tiny Spaces, which sold mini-cups, desks and couches perfectly suited for 8x6 New York City apartments. We sat on his tiny couch, drinking tiny cups of tea, saving the small amount of money we each had.

It took me almost an hour to reach his place from Queens, yet I still came and left every night. I walked down St. Mark's Place and thought of Rocker and the day we spent on that same street months before, rummaging through old CDs at vintage rock 'n' roll shops, back when everything was simple. In my happiest moments with Singer, I never once thought about Rocker, but as soon as I was alone, his memory perched on my shoulder and whispered sweet nothings into my ear. I lived in the past. I wondered if my heart would ever truly heal or if I would keep finding new people to fill in the gaps.

There's a phrase in every dancer's vocabulary called "muscle memory." When learning complex steps, we practice each move slowly and repeatedly, until it becomes natural to perform the steps in order. Similar to baking a cake, each step is an ingredient. After some mixing (hours of practicing), each ingredient comes together seamlessly into a routine. It always takes intense concentration for me to learn dance steps. I have to focus on every head, foot and body position, but eventually, the movement comes naturally as the memory of my muscles takes over. Instead of thinking about each step before I execute it, my body takes the reins. Muscle memory allowed me to be a Rockette and dance an eight-minute tap routine without worrying about the steps. I thought about what the person in the front row wore, what I planned on eating for dinner and the possibility of the earth blowing up, all at the same time. An invisible force let my body decide what it needed to do next.

My heart had its own muscle memory. It knew what to feel

and all the signs of attachment. The boy's name I tattooed on my heart changed, but the feelings were the same. Each time Singer complimented me or said something sweet, my heart reminded my brain of what it felt like to be happy. Almost instantly, it also reminded me of being hurt.

Winter in New York is the slowest audition season. From the small handful of auditions I was invited to, I booked an even smaller amount of jobs. I was hired to be a "hot girl" in a commercial for a beer I never heard of. The commercial required one day of shooting for a $450 buyout. I went back to go-go dancing at clubs around the city and at Bar Mitzvahs for $250 a night. Some weekends, I flew across America to judge junior dance competitions. I sat for 12 hours a day, watching teenagers perform the same way I did growing up: bright, fresh-faced and eager to please. They all dreamed of arriving in the big city and "making it." I smiled my biggest smile and told them about the awesomeness of being a professional dancer and how they should never give up. I hadn't the heart to explain that the life they chased was filled with so much struggle, heartbreak and rejection, that when they finally got there, they would wish for days like these, when their moms and dads brought them lunch in between numbers and when everyone received a medal just for showing up.

During the slow seasons in New York, no doesn't always mean no. The city that never sleeps took a break, and just because a director or producer didn't hire me, it only meant the timing wasn't right. At some point, you have to realize it isn't always about you. I sure did.

I believed the best thing I could do was continue to put myself out there. The bad thing about doing that is putting yourself in the direct line of fire for a whole lot of "no." But the wonderful thing is that you're also putting yourself in a miraculous place, living the life of your dreams.

When I wasn't unsuccessfully auditioning and working to make ends meet, I followed Singer and his band to their various gigs around town. I copied his CDs for my friends in the dance community. They adored his brand of heartfelt, scorned-love, melodic tunes.

Singer believed his own hype so much, I started believing it too. Small moments of triumph became part of my own list of why I thought Singer was so fantastic – he once played a concert with Gavin DeGraw, one New York City producer thought he was swell and he played one show at Joe's Pub, a popular spot slightly bigger than the closet-sized spaces where he normally performed. I focused so much on why he was great, I forgot to remind him, and myself, of all the outstanding things I offered in a relationship.

After hearing Singer's music, my dancer friends came to his shows and became his fans. I dated the music prom king, again. Only this prom king wore shoes with holes and couldn't afford to take me out to dinner. There was no gold crown in sight and certainly no car to take me home in. He had a serious case of LSD (aka lead singer disease) and his ego, talent and music infected everyone around him with wonderment. Fame, in all levels, is a sticky web. Even I had a hard time understanding my intentions.

Somewhere in the middle of trying to fool myself and everyone else around me that this was love, Rocker called me. Unexpectedly, he apologized for falling off the planet and breaking my heart. He told me he still wanted to marry me, and that I was the most perfect girl ever. His words were everything I wanted to hear, one year too late. But it was still nice to hear and helped heal my heart, I suppose. It's always nice to know when someone misses you. I spent my days feeding Singer's ego, and now a simple phone call from Rocker fed mine.

What is it about guys? They have a sick sixth sense. Some alarm must go off in their heads when they sense women are happy. Moved on. Not thinking about them 64 times a day. Why now do they need to "check in" and remind us they're not dead, which I fooled myself into assuming? Rocker was very much alive, existing and "sometimes" wondering about me.

When it comes to matters of the heart, nothing is ever going to make sense, but the best thing to do is cut out the romantic self-induced nonsense, along with all the toxic people. If someone says they care about you, love you, want to marry you, will always take care of you and then blatantly contradicts themselves, it's best to believe in the best parts about yourself and the worst parts about everyone else. There are amazing people to meet, know and love, but you won't ever see them if you keep focusing on the toxic, tragic train wrecks from the yesterdays of your love life.

I thanked Rocker for the phone call, and shook my head at the absurdity of it all.

I left Singer and the East Village especially late and walked toward the subway. Getting on the train, I realized it was far too late to take the long ride out to Queens by myself. Usually, I would ride in fear for 35 minutes and walk quickly back to my apartment without incident.

Somewhere between Queens Plaza and Kew Gardens, I sat in a subway car with only one other passenger, a strange man. He sat on the opposite end, and I tried my best to ignore the growls he sent me through his frothy mouth. He inched closer and purred at me like a cat, holding his hands out like claws. I stared

73

straight ahead, assuming he'd give up his taunting if I ignored him. I was wrong.

He sat down next to me, called me a "leopard," and pretended to rip the holes in my jeans with his "claws." He ogled me with the eyes of a truly crazy man. I wished for time to pass faster or for the train to speed up so we could reach the next station and I could run out of the car. Unfortunately, I was trapped inside the E train, more scared than ever before.

The man grabbed me and started to beat me, first grabbing my wrists and throwing me from side to side in the train. Then he grabbed my neck and pulled my face two inches from his own, not letting up until the doors opened and I could flee. It was weird how quiet I was during the attack. I was so scared, I couldn't even scream. I remember praying "please make him stop" repeatedly in my head. At the station, two police watchmen told me there was nothing they could do about the man, but offered to sit with me for the rest of my trip home. Frustrated and scared, I took a cab.

I couldn't eat for a week after the attack, partially from being afraid and also because I spent $45 on the cab ride home. When I told my friends about what happened, they were shocked and brought out their own arsenal of near-miss New York attacker stories. Every person who ever lived in New York City has one. Their story of the night the crazies came out and tried to beat, rob or taunt them. Where they walked from the subway to their front door with their keys in between their fingers just in case. My friends suggested I move to Manhattan, the only place I ever wanted to live, but couldn't afford. Another item on the list of things out of my reach – hearts, fame and a place to live with a decent area code.

I was sure I couldn't afford a better place, but I dragged a friend apartment shopping in Manhattan anyway. I found a few different options. The first, a 4x6 room with a sink, a twin bed and a window. The bathroom was located at the end of a plywood-covered hall, and shared by the 10 other apartments on the floor. I found out why they called the neighborhood "Hell's Kitchen." Another alternative, sleeping in someone's living room on a couch for $1,500 a month. I'd have to pull a shower curtain across my space when I needed to get dressed. I had little hope the next apartment would be any better. But when we arrived at the Upper West Side location, my faith was restored. I cried when I walked into the clean, newly renovated building at 209 West 97th Street.

A few weeks later, I moved into my first Manhattan apartment. I now lived in the tiny room of an apartment shared with four other young Manhattanites, surrounded by Jewish families and nail salons, squeezed between Central Park and the red line. My room cost $800 a month and was the size of a queen-sized mattress, but I had a doorman (if only from the hours of 4 to 10 p.m.) and a kitchen with a stove! Mostly, I got out of Queens, leaving behind the memories of subway beatings, damaged hearts and broken wombs. I lived on 97th Street and Broadway, which I took as a very good sign.

They say the neon lights are bright on Broadway.

They say there's always magic in the air.

Singer helped me assemble a twin-sized loft bed for my room. I literally ducked to use the rest of the space in my closet/bedroom. We used an IKEA wrench and worked all night, listening to Jeff Buckley's haunting rendition of "Last Goodbye," on repeat.

When we were done and Singer headed back to his place, I crawled into my semi-stable bed. I lay my head on a red pillow and stared at the ceiling, only a few inches away. I was so proud of myself. Here I was, little 'ol me, with a shiny new Manhattan address. I won the gold medal at the Olympics of life. Keltie Colleen: Undefeated Champion of Reinvention! For one moment, I forgot the sadness and pain from the loss I faced the previous year. For one moment, I understood the ability to make myself happy. But the moment was soon over, as my past came flooding back and I cried myself to sleep.

Chapter 7

Singer believed in God and was convinced "He" had big plans for me. God's plan sounded like a good thing. I still lived on avocados and nacho chips, was unemployed and felt seriously underwhelmed with any of my own plans. Singer invited me to church with him. I didn't know if it would help, but I needed something, anything to hold on to.

I woke up one Sunday morning and headed with him to a church in midtown Manhattan to meet God. I sat in the back row uncomfortably, surrounded by young families with children and Christian virgins wearing Abercrombie & Fitch jeans and summer dresses.

Singer was the worship leader, which meant he sang all of the songs during the sermon. My rock 'n' roll obsession turned heavenly, as I was now the world's first groupie who followed a guitar player to church. Instead of an invitation to the tour bus for a late, drink-filled night in a coffin bunk, there was an invitation to a group picnic with the rest of the church members in Central Park. I declined and went home. I took a sleeping pill and waited for the next day to come. God wasn't at church that day.

Spagatti organized a small "family" gathering at his place in Queens for the upcoming Easter holiday. Us New York dancer kids transplanted from all over Canada created a unique version of a modern family. My real family remained far away, separated by many time zones and miles, and I felt disconnected from them most of the time. Sometimes on purpose, because my brother's sickness hurt my heart, and rather than help, I selfishly followed my own dreams. I tried not to think about things at home. My fellow orphaned dancers and I created a support system in the tough world we chose. They were my family now. We cheered when there was a need to celebrate and cried on each other's shoulders when the pressures, struggles and disappointments were too much to stand. We gathered in our small apartments on holidays and being away from home became a little easier.

This dinner was no different, except now, Singer was a part of our family too. He got all the same hugs I did from my friends and at the end of the night, someone handed him a guitar and we had a family sing-along in the living room. After too much wine and too much food, we lay around the room, taking turns requesting songs for Singer to play. It started with Elton John's "Rocket Man" and ended with Singer's personal collection. Some people show off their cars, handbags or shoes – their symbol of where they belonged in the world. Mine was Singer. I had no faith in my own talent so I carried his around. Almost as good. Singer was my catch and with him, I showed the world I was OK after all. So many artists do this, and there's always a feeling behind our eyes that one day, everyone will find out that we're a sham. I was constantly worried that the world would find out I wasn't really a good dancer. But I was a good dancer. I was a Rockette. I was making strides. I danced my whole life. There wasn't some secret, like I had a body double and no talent. I felt that way most of the time, but it simply wasn't true. I didn't need to bring someone more talented around me to make me feel like my life was important. I was important on my own. I wouldn't realize this for another four years though, so at that time, Singer was my side dish of ego.

A few days later, I headed back to church for Easter Sunday. I asked my roommate to help me pick out an appropriate outfit. Turns out, I didn't own anything proper enough for the occasion. I went shopping and chose something to blend in with the other church-going girls in their white, conservative dresses. I felt like Julia Roberts in *Runaway Bride*. Whatever god the guy I dated followed, I followed. I was lost with absolutely no idea who I was. I tried to be the girl my boyfriend wanted so I didn't have to be alone. Singer wanted a nice church-going, white-dress-wearing, good girl, so I became that.

Once again, I sat in the back row while Singer sent his praises to God. Only this time, God found me. In the front of the room, a video projector flashed song lyrics. I gazed up and saw, "You are loved." My breath caught in my throat. I will never know if those were just the words Singer sang or if it was a sign from God, but it was time to give up my pity party. So many of my choices were because I tried too hard to get everyone to love me, but didn't love any parts of myself.

There was one sin Singer was most against. We could kiss, but it always stopped there. I never met anyone who didn't try to involve me in a super make out session after a few days. I struggled to understand Singer's actions. Either he was considerate, caring and understood how Rocker dragged me through the mud, or he was an honest Christian who believed God would strike him down if he looked at my boobs, or maybe he was gay. All three ideas swam in my head.

My friends thought it was strange, but I told them of my vow of celibacy. I thought I found my perfect match: a musician, possibly gay, who wore Chuck Taylors, had shaggy hair and wouldn't pressure me to do anything I didn't want to!

Our relationship seemed perfect until one night, while we were walking down the street, I turned to him and said, "I think I'm falling in love with you." Singer stared at me for a few seconds and then continued ahead, saying, "That's nice."

So far away from being in love with him, it was a ridiculous thing to say. I wanted to be in love so badly and would have given anything to hear the words, "I love you," even if they were a lie. But lying was a sin, so Singer didn't say it back. I knew I wasn't in love with him, but still felt defeated.

Chapter 8

The Rockettes have an interesting rehiring policy. When the season ends each year, they publish a 60 percent list, which means 60 percent of the Rockettes they need for the next season are automatically rehired. The day the "list" goes out is the busiest day of the year. Rockettes call each other to congratulate, offer condolences and attempt to figure out the thought process behind who made it and who didn't. The reason the day holds so much power is that the system used for rehiring is completely wacky. There's nothing mathematical or fair about how they choose the list. You can be a star Rockette one year, making the list, doing all the special events and then show up to audition the next year and are given the cold shoulder. The feedback is always the same: "Work on your tap." Rockettes cry, gossip and make plans for the next year based on this list. The remaining 40 percent (the "Reject Rockettes") have to re-audition for their spots. They fly to New York or Los Angeles and audition in tights and a leotard for a panel of directors who saw them in tights and a leotard every day for the past six months. No one really needs to "work on their tap" if they're good enough to do the show more than two years. There's really no reason to not rehire someone unless they really messed up. Which I did.

The prior year, I was an automatic rehire aka "Good

Rockette," and this year I was a "Reject Rockette." After my drunken and depressed Christmas kicking season, I wasn't surprised. I was forced to show up at Radio City Music Hall to re-audition for a job I already held for the previous two years. I couldn't remember the last time I took a dance class. I was bloated, pale and severely out of shape. I spent so much time following Singer around Manhattan, I forgot to follow my own dreams. It must've showed because on the day the rehire phone calls went out, I didn't receive one. No list. Bad audition. No job.

I waited until 9 p.m. the next day before I called my Rockette sisters to see if they received calls. They all did. Was there a terrible mistake? I examined my phone to be sure it worked properly. I checked and rechecked my voicemail, thinking I missed something. My worst fear was confirmed when I received an e-mail from the Rockette administrator saying all calls were made and there was no mistake. There was no place for me in the line that year. I wouldn't be a Rockette.

Devastated, I reacted how I normally did when things fell apart. I got dressed up, went to see Singer play and drank six glasses of wine in less than 30 minutes. As soon as he got off stage, I fell into his arms and cried hysterically. I screamed that I didn't know why I wasn't rehired. Singer had to drag me out of the venue after his show that night, which should've been my first clue. Before he could guide my drunken body into a cab, I fell into the gutter and couldn't stand up again. I was a mess, inside and out. I knew I didn't deserve the job. I cried for the loss of the best thing to ever happen to me. It was completely my own fault. I hated myself.

I woke up the next morning unsure of how I got home. I felt like my beverage of choice the night before was "Nail Polish Remover Martini." My insides were rotten, my mouth was dry and my head pounded. It was time to make a change. A big one. In the mirror, rockbottom stared back at me in the yellows of my eyes. I took a leap of faith and peeled off my bitter boots. I attended as many dance classes as I possibly could. I drank only water. I detoxed my life, again.

Rockbottom is the point where you can't make excuses for yourself and in the deepest part of your soul, you know you're not OK. It's easy to get there when you're used to lying. I convinced myself I was fine, but repeatedly, my actions disproved this. Telling lies to other people is unfair and cruel. Telling lies to yourself and believing them is borderline psychotic.

I was determined to prove to myself that I was better than this. I was inspired by the people back home, by the people who hadn't hired me for another Rockette season, and of course, by Singer, who watched closely for my reaction to my crash into rockbottomness. I was at such a low, I could only go up again. I waited for someone or something to throw me a rope to help me climb out of my despair. The cleaner my body got and the clearer my mind became, it became obvious no one would rescue me. I needed to find my own way to crawl out.

And trust me, I crawled, fought tooth and nail and dragged every inch of my body into the light. Crawling out of rockbottom meant staring at my bloated and out of shape body in wall-length mirrors, for two hours at a time in the multiple dance classes I attended each day. It meant hours of solitude after turning down friends who invited me to parties where there would be liquor. It meant grocery shopping for healthy fuel for my body, instead of grabbing whatever sweets were on the counter at the corner deli. It meant long walks alone in Central Park, the wind biting at my nose, ears and heart. I sat with the ghost of John Lennon at Strawberry Fields and pictured the fascinating world I wanted to exist around me. Maybe if I sat long enough with the panhandlers and hippies at the "Imagine" memorial, I would walk away with bright, psychedelic reds and blues painted across the sky. My gloomy grays would be erased. I felt strong, beautiful and ready to reinvent myself.

I planned a new path and jumped back into the dance audition world feverishly. Only this time, the universe rewarded my fresh outlook. A big-budget Disney movie, *Enchanted*, was auditioning dancers. I was called in for the ballroom scene and spent the entire day faking my way through my best version of the Viennese Waltz. I was cut. The next day, I was called in for the "kicking girls" scene and advanced to the end of the audition. After kicking for six hours, I was cut again. I was called in a third time for the bride scene. I laughed as I showed up in the same leotard I wore for the last two days.

The choreographer sat behind the director's table, its surface covered with scattered headshots, resumes and notepads. Before my turn to dance, I jokingly said, "I'm going to keep coming back until you hire me." She giggled. The director giggled. Once again, my charm won me a job over my mediocre talent. The dance portion of my life upturned and I was cast as one of the principal dancers in the film.

Enchanted was shot in New York City and every dancer wanted to book it. I was one of 10 selected to learn a complex string of lifts for a performance in the middle of Central Park, in the middle of the summer, in the middle of the biggest dance extravaganza of the decade.

My self-esteem still took a beating. The choreographer dished out instructions at rehearsals, and I could barely look her in the eye. My partner was tall, handsome and one of her favorite male dancers in the city. I was clumsy and nervous. Normally I'm great at partnering – svelte, light and strong, with all the makings of a great adagio. The choreographer wasn't impressed. Her eyes burned through my head as she glared at me. Her brain probably processed thoughts of regrets and wishes that she hadn't cast me. But the contracts were signed and there I was, awkwardly trying to stay afloat in the sky above my partner's arms.

The next week, all the dancers rehearsed inside Roseland Ballroom. The scene was massive and all 150 dancers practiced in one room. The team of directors and choreographers marched around, moving dancers, making changes, shouting orders and running choreography. It was the biggest production rehearsal I was ever a part of.

I stood in my place, scanning the giant circle of dance, silent and focused, when the choreographer grabbed my hips from behind. She wanted to move me from my position and pulled me to a new spot. Taken aback, I fell over my own feet and dug the heel of my shoe directly into her foot. Even though it was an accident, it didn't matter. She shot me a look of death and barked at her assistant to tell "that one" where to go. For the rest of the month-long shoot, she wore her foot wrapped in gauze and limped around the set. She never hired me again.

We filmed the scenes in a beautiful summer in Central Park, and as with any New York production, with an entire city of spectators. I glowed in a huge, puffy wedding dress. I invited Singer to see me in action at any time during my week of 12-hour shoot days. Despite all of the drama in rehearsals, I was so excited to film my first movie and I wanted Singer to be just as excited! The dreams we spent so many nights talking about while sipping tiny cups of tea were finally coming true.

Singer never showed. He was always busy with something more important. He was great at telling me all the things I needed to do to get my life back on track, but never wanted to celebrate any of my successes. Maybe he was jealous because things started to go well for me. Maybe he liked being the strong, put-together man to the mess of a woman he constantly had to save. When I wasn't falling, he didn't need me. I was disappointed. The old taste of heartbreak soured my tongue. Still numb from the prior summer with Rocker, I barely felt Singer break my heart. His actions were another small beating to the already pulverized piece of me.

Singer headed back into the studio to work on a new record and his bright future. He hibernated in his cave off 10th Avenue and I wouldn't see him for days. Sometimes, I stopped by and sat quietly on the leather couch while he played. He talked self-indulgently about his snare drums and snaps, completely ignoring me. After a while, he started to ignore me outside of the studio as well. The number of phone calls dwindled. I stopped going to church with him.

Our relationship was over, but neither of us wanted to be the bad guy. He didn't want to say the words, and I put up with being treated like garbage because I didn't want to be alone. I was always alone though. Singer was never my true partner – he was an equally self-centered struggling artist who needed something to cling to when nothing happened with his music. I was an afterthought. He knew it, I knew it, but we were both too lonely and busy to find something healthier. I didn't lose every ounce of myself inside the disappointment. I was a woman who wanted it all. Women are amazing creatures who love, live, feel, hurt, hug, laugh, kneel, skip and be. I'm not sure why the universe doesn't hand out gold medals just for being a woman and deciphering the maze of feelings, emotions, hormones, mirrors and shoulda-coulda-wouldas of everyday life – but it should start. We deserve it.

A male friend once said to me in passing, "Vulnerable girls are so attractive." I wondered if that was my problem. In the past, I never allowed anyone I dated to see my fears or insecurities. I only showed happy emotions, building up a façade of strength and confidence. Many times, I didn't feel that way, but I was under the impression this was how I needed to be. I was a big, grown-up girl and my copy of *Why Men Love Bitches* taught me to only let men see what I wanted them to see and conceal the rest.

It was funny, I guess. A few of my friends received the, "I don't want a girlfriend right now" kiss off around the same time my relationship with Singer ended. These were strong, assertive women with their own awesome careers, lives and futures. Weeks later, it seemed like these guys did want girlfriends. Only, the girls they wanted were ones with nothing better to do than follow their guy around, agreeing with everything he said and living their lives for him instead of themselves.

Maybe this is why Singer liked me so much in the beginning. I was happy to be his groupie and follow him around New York

City like a rat on garbage night. I was so broken when I met him that all I wanted was to be liked. I tossed my own ambitions to the wayside and was easy to keep around because I stopped living my own life. I became the female version of him and he loved it. When I finally found the balls to get back up onto my own dream horse, things fell apart.

Spagatti and I ate dinner in the East Village and I complained about my falling out with Singer. Our group of artist friends was enamored with his music and never said a bad thing about him, but I could always be honest with Spagatti. He informed me from the start that he didn't like the idea of Singer and believed he'd hurt me all along. He said Singer was selfish. At the beginning of our six-month relationship, I didn't agree, but I sure did now. Spagatti was right – he always is.

Maybe I scared Singer. Maybe the fact I didn't want to follow him around anymore made me unattractive. Maybe learning to take care of myself, moving into Manhattan and getting back into my career freaked him out. I had my own money, career and life again. I rarely needed his help and maybe that made me ugly. Singer liking only the tragic, messy and depressed version of me bummed me out. I worked so hard on learning from my mistakes and healing that I never imagined it could be a bad thing. My growth gave his ego a run for its money. He needed to grow too and get his life together.

Singer lived in a village of uncertainty and when I tried to fit myself in his life, Keltietown was nowhere on his map. He picked me up along the way. My broken and sad self helped keep him going by telling him how great he was. When I became great independently, I wasn't useful anymore. I became a sub-chapter in the least important part of his story, so I closed the book and got out.

I scanned Central Park from my little window on the Upper West Side, and wondered why someone wouldn't want a beautiful, fun, successful, sweet girl to spend time with. Why did I work so hard on being enlightened if guys always wanted girls who strolled through life without purpose? It seemed backward. But I couldn't expect anything less from the complicated male species.

The strongest disappointments happen when we set high expectations for ourselves. If I was OK with being a floater in life and dance, I wouldn't be upset. But I expected so much of myself and from my body that when people find flaws, I have a hard time accepting it. Some days, I feel like the worst dancer. Some days, I feel like the most unattractive and least lovable woman. I'm far away from being the best dancer or the most beautiful, but I'd like to think I can hold my own somewhere in the middle of the pack.

I kept setting myself up for disappointment, and my relationship with Singer taught me another lesson. People who fail you once will most likely continue to do so. I like to think people change and grow, or somehow, "I'm sorry," can mean, "I still love you," when, in fact, it only means, "Please don't hate me as much as I hate myself."

My problem stems from never truly hating anyone or anything. Singer was an idealist. He loved to write songs about happy endings, but he didn't want to work on creating them for himself. What I wish he could have realized, and what we all should realize, is life isn't something that's thrown at us. It's something we create. You control your own destiny and if you want a happy ending, it's yours to hold. You just have to be willing to work for it.

We're defined in life not by what we say, but what we do. It's easy to make promises, but it's hard to keep them. It's easy to say you want to be a good person, but it takes effort to actually be good. It's easy to say you adore someone, but it's spectacular when you actually do. It's important for everyone to realize how it's extremely easy to talk about who you are, but it's a harder battle to actually be that person.

Singer taught me not to listen to what people say to me, but what their actions say. Someone who adores you will make it clear they adore you. You deserve to be adored.

People are afraid of happy endings because they're too sad and unsure of themselves. They don't believe they deserve one. Singer and I differed because I knew I deserved a happy ending. After wallowing in sadness, I created a wonderful light in my life. I hoped one day, a fellow with his own light would become my Prince Charming.

I refused to give up on that dream or myself, but I gave up on Singer. One more notch on my tight jeaned, guitar playing battlefield of loves. I waved my white flag, and I walked away.

PART THREE: THE DREAMER

Chapter 9

People say the third time's a charm. In my case, not so much.

MTV's Video Music Awards were being hosted at Radio City Music Hall. Many "danceable" artists were on the bill, and the buzz around the dance community was huge because MTV planned to hire local dancers. My agent called me in for three auditions. I went to three auditions. I got cut from three auditions.

At the last minute, my agent called again with a fourth audition. I asked her what I should wear since I never heard of the band I'd be dancing for. I searched their songs on YouTube, deciding to wear my most rock 'n' roll outfit, complete with Chuck Taylors.

Dancers salivated with their last hopes for the MTV stage. Everyone wanted this job and luckily, I was hired and started rehearsals the next day. We dressed in burlesque, *Moulin Rouge* costumes and the choreography was thrashy, sexy and tons of fun. I loved it.

A few days before the show, the band came to Chelsea studios and watched us rehearse. The lead singer's pants were tight and he wore Reebok high-top sneakers, while the other three wore fancy, pointed-toe Beatle boots. They all looked about 14 years old, nervous to be a few feet away from the sexy dancers romping around to their music. They drank Starbucks on the floor while managers and bodyguards whizzed around them. Apparently, they were the new hot thing and everyone cared. I still hadn't heard of them but exclaimed enthusiastically to an MTV cameraman that I was "sooooo excited" to be dancing for them.

On the day of the show, the band's manager called my agent to invite me to the after party. I figured all the dancers were invited. Later, I realized one of the guys in the band noticed me at rehearsal and thought I was cute. Another thing rockstars don't have to do for themselves – ask a girl out.

Everyone who was anyone hung out backstage at Radio City that night. I overheard tour stories from Justin Timberlake and Beyonce's dancers in between make-up chairs and wardrobe tents. I knew almost everyone in the room. Some of my friends danced for Shakira, others for Missy Elliott. I clutched my backstage pass like a million dollars. I grew up watching the VMAs and was beside myself as I stared at my reflection in a mirror. My clip-on hair extensions were blonde and perfectly curled. My make-up was expertly applied by someone dressed in black. My costume was an original from a collection at the Metropolitan Opera House. In a few hours, I would dance at the MTV VMAs for the first time and was exactly where I wanted to be. That night was one of the only times I felt as strong and beautiful as an entire glam squad made me look.

I'll never forget whipping my hair and throwing my huge crinoline dress around the stage. I danced in front of the biggest stars. Pink sat in the fifth row, and I recalled the numerous times I listened to "Just Like a Pill" on the treadmill when I was crawling out of my rockbottom. Backstage, I wished the band luck on their nominations after the performance. The skinniest one ignored my comments but asked if I planned on attending the after party.

After the show, I headed downtown. I was still semi-broke and wore black jeans, a black tank and a pleather belt. I was so uncool. I called my mom on the way to ask if she saw me on television. She said I looked amazing in my black and white dress – I wore purple. Typical. Dancers work for a week and are shown for maybe 20 seconds total, so even the woman who birthed you can't pick you out. I was a little disappointed but didn't let it get me down. I was ready for some fun at the first after party where my name was actually on the list.

Awkwardly, I approached the band at the bar. I said hello to the thin, frail, beautiful boy beside me. He said he was waiting to talk to me all night. He was the reason for the invite. He offered me a drink, which I declined. He told me he never had a drink before and didn't plan on having one. I liked this boy. He wore shiny black boots and there wasn't a Chuck Taylor in sight. The boy looked uncomfortable with his newfound fame, which I found endearing.

From the moment we started talking, I felt connected to him. He was sweet and slightly odd, like a strange bird in the zoo you can't help but stare at because you've never seen anything else like it. Everything out of his mouth belonged in some wild romantic comedy filled with modern-day Romeos and beautiful love songs. He existed in the present but didn't actually live here with the rest of us. He was a starry-eyed dreamer who created an entire world in his head. Instead of dealing with the not-so-magical situations in his life, his mind transformed to a place where he was happy. His dreams consisted of haunting melodies, men in fanciful 1800s suits and a blissful utopia where people fell deeply in love. I had a hard time believing there was someone who spent more time inside their head than I did, but here he was. My heart fluttered with the hope that I finally met my match – The Dreamer.

You know that strange, tingling feeling in the pit of your stomach when something is so exciting it threatens to spill out of your mouth and ears? That's how I felt. I liked him and tried to act cool, but was obviously a huge dork. When confronted with social situations I can't handle, I find a way to pull myself out. I decided to leave the party and suggested we exchange phone numbers. I took out my phone but couldn't remember what

Dreamer introduced himself as. "Brian?" I asked. He laughed and corrected me. "You really don't know who I am, do you?"

Dreamer texted me as soon as I left the party, and I felt like I was thrown back into high school. Nervous butterflies fluttered in my stomach, and I couldn't stop giggling at his silly responses. Assuming he was a flirt, it never occurred to me that he was actually still a child. As I got older, the age of the men I found attractive stayed the same. Gorgeous rockers I fell for were always 20-year-olds.

Dreamer said he left the party after I did and invited me back to his hotel. I never did the after-after party thing before, but the night turned into something thrilling. I recalled the conversation with my mother earlier where she said, "Enjoy every minute and stay out all night!" If I went, I'd only be doing what my mom told me to, which justified my decision to agree to a late hotel date.

In his suite, we ordered room service. I told him about filming *Enchanted* in Central Park and how fabulous it was, as if my one background dance scene in a feature film increased my level of dateability. I fidgeted nervously on his bed, unable to look at his baby face for too long. Christian Dior and Louis Vuitton bags cluttered the floor and I wore a $4 belt from Rainbow on 14th Street. Had I really spent hours picking out the perfect outfit for a VMA after party, only to choose a cheap pleather belt as the best option? We were both out of our league for completely different reasons. People who surround themselves with fancy things usually have a strong desire to feel like they belong. What he didn't realize is that I was a co-dependent perfectionist who would seduce, date and fall in love with him without his consent. While we ate our ham and egg sandwiches, I wish I knew that we were at the start of a beautiful and ultimately tragic love story.

Again, my brain told me to run the other way because Dreamer was my type and my type never worked for me. As usual, my brain lost out to the overwhelming desires of my heart. I stayed and smiled, enjoying what I thought would be the only time I'd set foot in a place as elaborate as Trump Towers. When we finished our food, we still sat on opposite sides of the bed. I had a feeling he expected us to hook up. Feeling uncomfortable, I decided to take control. I wanted us to be somewhere relaxing, somewhere less classy and more New Yorky. Somewhere I could get a delicious mug of green tea.

I took Dreamer on his very first New York City taxi ride to my Upper West Side apartment. Then, I did what I do best: made tea and watched myself on television. I asked Dreamer if he should be somewhere else – perhaps partying with strippers, on a night where his band won the biggest award of that year's show. He informed me that he had never been to a strip club. His innocence was adorable and believable. I thought his good-natured personality kept him from associating with that kind of garbage. In actuality, it was because he wasn't of legal drinking age and had hard time passing for 14, let alone 21. He hadn't begun his life of experimentation, one that, for me, was almost over by the age of 20. It wasn't that partying wasn't his thing, he just wasn't exposed to its sweet and sinful aroma yet.

Until 6:30 a.m., we sat on a couch covered in dog hair and watched our amazing performance more than 30 times. Dreamer had to fly back to his hometown of Las Vegas, and when he kissed me on the stoop of my apartment building, I never wanted it to end. We kissed as taxis surrounded us, store gates opened and professionals in suits rushed to work, but none of that mattered. It was the most perfect kiss I ever experienced. I had no idea if I would ever see him again, but for the moment, I reveled in the sweetness of our innocent kiss. I found out everything I needed to know about him with that kiss. Words were useless. I knew it. He knew it. This was it.

I told Spagatti about my crazy night. "Do what you want, Keltie," he said, "but he *is* going to hurt you." I didn't believe him, but again, I was wrong.

Dreamer and I were technologically joined at the hip after that first night. The week after the VMAs, we obsessed over each other and shared every detail of our lives through text messages. Once that began, I didn't put my phone down for almost three years. I was famous throughout my circle of friends for always being on my phone. One of my girlfriends actually dressed up as me for Halloween that year and just wore normal clothes and walked around with a Sidekick. Dating in the age of technology is about having love in your heart and a cell phone in your hand.

I booked a gig in the Meatpacking District and on a break, I called Dreamer. Our conversation turned into discussing the next time we might see each other, and I asked him if he still lived with his parents in Las Vegas. He told me that his dad passed away a few weeks prior. I stopped in the middle of the street, and even with the loud honks and street noise, I could only hear the sound of my insides churning. I didn't know what to say. I asked him what happened, and he said his father drank himself to death. I mumbled something about church and his dad looking down on him from heaven, proud of his son for being so amazing and successful. Dreamer doubted his father ended up in heaven. Our conversation was heavy and awful. My heart broke for him. Now I understood why a night without alcohol at the VMAs seemed like a relief for him.

I had a plan. The object of my affection was living in Las Vegas and coincidentally, so was one of my best girlfriends. I organized a trip to Nevada. I visited my friend and went on my first official date with Dreamer. I'm really good at forcing fate sometimes, and there was a good chance I may have never seen him again, had I not orchestrated this trip. I jumped into a relationship with him the same way I attended my dance auditions, by making sure I was in the right place at the right time (with the right outfit on).

For our first date, we met on the strip for the Cirque du Soleil show, *Zumanity*. My hands were shaking and sweating from being around him. I had no idea what to expect from our date. Dates are like auditions, sometimes you get a callback and sometimes you just have to try again another time. Despite the weirdness, I hoped for a callback with Dreamer.

Later that night, he offered to drive me home. When we arrived in the parking garage, he directed me toward an old red Ford Taurus that had one of the windows duct taped together. He apologized profusely for not having a nicer car. His life of Trump Tower hotel stays and Dior jackets didn't yet trickle down to his life in Las Vegas. There, he was still normal, no one fawned over him, dressed him or followed him around, yet. He was an average teenager with a beat up car, trying to impress a girl on their first date.

I couldn't remember where my friend lived or what streets to follow. We drove around Las Vegas all night in his old car, searching for an unknown address and frequently pulling over just to make out. I felt like a silly, happy and renewed child. All the torture my heart went through the past few years fell so carelessly. Dreamer was innocent and there was no way someone so sweet and unsure of himself could ever hurt me. Rocker oozed confidence and shouted whatever he wanted to say. Dreamer was impeccable with his words, intent and sincere.

The next night, Dreamer took me out to dinner at a loud,

family-filled Mexican joint for date number two. He wore more make-up than I did. Unromantic and awkward, we were probably the two nerdiest people on the planet. I was hooked.

I begrudgingly returned to life in New York unsure what to do with myself. For the first time in two years, I wouldn't be joining my Rockette sisters on the road. I ran out of options and in a last ditch effort to do something with my year, I auditioned to dance for the New York Knicks at Madison Square Garden. I was chosen for the team and they gave me a plastic backpack and a tank top. I forced myself to appear excited when I told my friends, but I couldn't help comparing the backpack to the iPod and Tiffany jewelry I received from the Rockettes. I felt like I took a giant step backward.

I was once a part of the world's most famous precision dancers, and now I'd be doing booty pops for drunken sports spectators. I wouldn't know until later, but being on the Knicks dance squad opened more doors than I could've imagined. I met some of my best friends and traveled around the world, seeing places some people only dream of. I was wrong about the Knicks the same way I was wrong about most things I delved into that year.

Rehearsals started, and I dove into the world of sports entertainment, selling sex as dance and working hard for almost no money. I only spoke of Dreamer. Overnight, my whole self became defined by what was going on between the two of us. He would return to New York in a few weeks, and I counted down the days, planned the outfits, repeated cute text messages and fantasized about our new life together. There's an eternal flaw in my programming that allows me to create nonexistent moments. I fall so hard with the idea of someone that I never take the time to determine if this person is the right choice for me. Something inside me decides this is it and I spend all of my energy making sure it lives up to the image I create in my head. It's a dangerous game to mix fantasy with reality, and I'm usually the one who gets hurt.

In addition to dancing for the Knicks, I also rehearsed for the highly-anticipated workshop for Jerry Mitchell's new project. Jerry Mitchell was the most adored director on Broadway. He was famous in New York and everyone would kill to work for him. Things were looking up. Even with my exhausting schedule, I barely slept for the entire four days Dreamer was in town.

Being around him turned me into a silly 14-year-old girl. I felt
a sense of camaraderie with the actual 14-year-old girls who
screamed during his concert.

Dreamer was staying at the W Hotel. We spent most of our
evenings in bed, eating room service, talking about our lives
and learning more about each other's deepest, darkest places.
We stayed under the safe haven of our blankets, sharing secrets.
When he left to fly to Europe, I stayed in bed. The sheets smelled
like him. He texted me on the way to the airport, "I think some
butterflies just flew out of my mouth." I wasn't exactly sure
what he meant, but I knew it was a good thing. Everything he
did and said was artistic. He never said I was pretty, but instead
compared my face to the night sky. Dating him was like being the
ingénue in one of my favorite Broadway musicals. He spoke in
the language of epic.

Dreamer and I being apart was almost too much for us
to bear. I defied our eight hour time difference, and instant
messaged sweet nothings to my sweet something. I couldn't stand
being away from him. During our "honeymoon stage," we spent
so much time apart, my obsession with him worsened. I worked
and kept busy, but he danced in the back of my mind all day.

I decided to visit him on tour in Europe. In addition to that
month's rent, I had $1,300 to my name. I booked a flight to
London for $1,000. The only catch was that I would be flying on
Air India, which I never heard of before.

For an airline to exist, it had to be safe, right? Stepping on
the plane was like walking into a 1970s curry cook-off. Dirty
and yellow, the jet's walls showed signs of age after many years of
passengers smoking on their way across the ocean. The plane was
packed, and I was sure Dreamer would be repulsed by me when I
got off the plane.

When I finally I arrived in London, I had no idea where I was going or where I was staying. Dreamer's tour bus didn't roll into town until the next day, so I gave myself time to roam around London and be a tourist. I met a guy at the airport who offered to sit beside me on the train and help me get off at the right station. We chatted and he offered me a place to shower and get freshened up before I started exploring. This never seemed odd to me. I have a naïve tendency to trust people. I think, "I'm nice, so you must be too." Luckily this charming Englishman stayed true to his word, gave me a cup of coffee, a shower and helped me on my way. That day, I toured all around London. I was completely fearless. I walked around with my backpack, clicked my camera and ate delicious chocolate that reminded me of my home in Canada.

Halfway through the afternoon, I remembered I didn't have anywhere to sleep. I planned to meet up with an old photographer friend, but my phone wasn't calling the number he gave me. I found a park bench and thought about my options. I could get a hotel with the last $300 in my bank account, sleep on the park bench or try to find the nice Englishman's apartment from earlier. Another young British man sat down next to me and struck up a conversation. I told him about my plan to meet my guy the next day and explained that he was a touring musician. He asked me where Dreamer was that night. I explained he was in Brussels and how I couldn't get a cheap flight from New York City to Belgium so I flew to London instead, and now had nowhere to sleep. He laughed and informed me that Brussels was only two hours by train, so I could hop on the Eurostar that evening to see my man. I never knew the guy's name, but I'm sure he giggled as I skipped toward the train station. I was going to Brussels!

I arrived in Brussels that evening. The city was quaint, dimly lit and none of the signs were in English. I tried to locate the address of the venue and was surprised when I saw the red tour bus in front of me. The venue looked like a dive bar in New York, and I would've missed it if the bus wasn't out front. I spotted Dreamer's bodyguard and he reached out to take my luggage aboard. I handed him my backpack and he laughed. "Is this all you've got?" he asked. I was in Europe for a week, and I only brought a pair of jeans, three t-shirts and a pair of boots. I traveled to Europe with nowhere to sleep, on an airline I never heard of, to see a guy I barely knew. Obviously, I knew what my priorities were.

The next night back in London, I realized people were watching me. I ordered a sandwich in a shop by Dreamer's venue, and a group of young girls overheard my accent and asked if I was American. They asked why I was in London, and I told them I dated a guy in a band playing around the corner that night. I then noticed Dreamer's face on the girls' t-shirts. What happened next involved screaming, questions and a group of the cutest English girls following me back to the venue to see what door I would go in. I honestly never realized what was going on. I was inside show business my entire life, so backstages, managers and shows were normal to me. It never occurred to me that some of these girls lived and breathed every moment to see the backstage of a venue or the inside of a tour bus. I watched the four boys eat leftover pizza and share a tiny one-room dressing room and the same dingy stall of a shower that wasn't anywhere as glamorous or interesting as the young sandwich shop girls assumed it was. To be honest, it was actually quite boring, and if it wasn't for Dreamer's eyes staring back at me, I most likely would've fallen asleep.

As I boarded my plane home, I found a note inside my bag from Dreamer: "Thank you for coming to visit me. You are such an amazing girl, and I keep finding out more reasons why." I clutched onto the note the entire curry-filled flight home. I arrived back in New York City completely broke and totally rich.

Chapter 10

Madison Square Garden is an extraordinary place. Musical artists and athletes dream of sharing their talents to a sold-out crowd inside the Garden. I just worked there. The Knicks City Dancers are the pride and joy of any game, and of course, New York City sports fans. To my surprise, running onto the court to dance for 20,000 screaming fans was intense, exciting and fulfilling. One night in December, the Garden hosted two perfect events: upstairs in the arena was a Knicks vs. Lakers basketball game and downstairs in the theater was the New York stop on Dreamer's band's tour. For me, the bigger event happened in the smaller venue. I disregarded the fact that I was a Knicks dancer performing to a sold-out crowd that night. All that mattered was Dreamer one floor beneath me, playing to a third of the crowd. Regardless, I was proud of him. I had the sound guy at the Knicks game play one of Dreamer's songs during the time out. I annoyed every girl in the dressing room by talking about my fabulous life and this amazing coincidence. I nauseated everyone with my happiness.

After our double shows, I met Dreamer in his dressing room and we made our first public appearance together. It only lasted a minute but for us to walk hand-in-hand from the doors of Madison Square Garden to the waiting taxicab his bodyguard hailed for us was enough. We were together for months and no one knew. That moment, people started speculating and stalking "the blonde girl" holding hands with Dreamer. People wanted to find out my name, my story and any reason to hate me. The object of my affection was the object of their obsession. I would've hated me too.

We took a cab uptown to the hotel the band stayed at. It happened to be called The Dream. Ironic, since I was living out most girls' fantasies by staying there with him. Dreamer turned to me and asked, "Will you be my girlfriend?" I stopped. I might have gagged. I really liked Dreamer, but I had such terrible luck with boyfriends. I loved being together without any rules or titles. I reached a point in my life where I expected everyone to break their promises to me and figured that if I stayed out of situations involving any, I wouldn't get hurt. I was like a child who finally learned that if you stick your hand in the fire, you're going to get burned. But lying beside his soft skin in that magical hotel, drenched in candle light and with the grumbling of Manhattan taxicabs as our soundtrack, I could only look in his little puppy dog eyes and say, "Yes." And just like that, I had another musician boyfriend. I was convinced he was different than the others because in those months, he was. But he wouldn't always be.

The next thing I knew, my body broke out in big, red, itchy hives. I convinced myself it was an allergic reaction to the bed sheets, when really, my heart was probably trying to tell me something. It sent a signal through my bloodstream, to every inch of my body so I received the message loud and clear. The huge, blotchy hives were a physical reaction to my emotional chaos. I literally repelled commitment.

In addition to my new relationship, my dance life was also on the upswing. When I wasn't dancing for the Knicks, I met with

new choreographers and auditioned. I appeared on Saturday
Night Live, 30 Rock and in a handful of music videos. I was so
busy that when my agent told me I booked the latest iPod ad, I
had to turn it down. I used all of my vacation time from the
Knicks to see Dreamer in Europe and wasn't allowed to miss
another game. I lost out on a huge contract. At the time, I didn't
care because it seemed completely worth it. It wasn't. I was so
intent on being with Dreamer that I made poor, irresponsible
choices. I worked so hard to make it in New York and all of a
sudden, my whole world revolved around Dreamer, being with
him, taking care of him, saving him from himself. He was my
boyfriend and my pet project. I wasn't working on my career, I
was working on "us." To say I was distracted was an
understatement.

I floated around the city, and counted down the days until his
next visit. He was set to arrive in New York to be photographed
for an upcoming cover of *Rolling Stone* magazine. It was strange
to say that, and coming out of my mouth I could've said,
"Dreamer is coming to New York City to eat a sandwich." I never
understood the power of his rise to fame. To me, he was just
Dreamer, insecure, always muddling on some sort of instrument
and the guy who adored me.

The first night he arrived, he looked me straight in the eye
and said, "I'm in love with you." I gasped and turned pale. It was a
terrible reaction. I was so afraid of love that I severed that part of
my being. I cut off the life flow to the part of my heart
responsible for real love and forgot about my hopes for my own
fairytale ending. My mind raced to find a response. I blinked as
the moments passed. When I finally opened my mouth, the only
words that came out were, "Thank you."

Dreamer's tour was a huge success and whenever I could, I

made it out on the road to spend time with him. His tour bus was different than anything I experienced on the road with Rocker. The cabinets were stocked with M&M's and cookies. The fridge was filled with Capri Sun and the bus was spotless. It resembled my grandma's kitchen more than a rock 'n' roll tour bus.

One night, Dreamer and I watched some of the opening bands. We stood backstage, slow dancing to other bands' songs. No one saw us, and it was one of the sweetest moments we ever had. Being with Dreamer was like being a part of the best moments of every love story. Some people are lucky if they experience one of the romantic things Dreamer did for me. He was shy toward expressing these feelings in front of other people but when it was just the two of us, somewhere the rest of the world couldn't get in, the truth came out.

Dreamer talked about me on television. Someone asked him what his favorite thing was about me was and he answered live, in front of a huge audience, "She never gets jealous." He confirmed to the millions of teenage fans that he was taken. I think I was the only happy fan that day. What I didn't know was that my life was about to be turned upside down by complete strangers, the power of the Internet and cruel gossip. I felt like the target of every girl in America who didn't understand why Dreamer chose to be with me. To others, I was a ditzy cheerleader trying to get ahead in the business. Really, I was someone affected, introspective and falling in love.

While walking down the New York City streets every day, his face greeted me from the covers of music magazines. I bought them all to support him. His *Rolling Stone* issue came out and in his interview, he said he was dating a "nice" girl. I was in shock to even make it into the article. Years later, when I finally hit another rockbottom, "nice" became a dirty word at my therapy sessions.

Being nice is one thing, being so nice that I allowed everyone to walk all over me was another.

Christmas in New York was stunning. After celebrating so many Christmases in hotel rooms on tour with the Rockettes, I was excited to spend the holidays at my apartment. I bought a tree, wrapped presents and counted down the days until Dreamer arrived to spend Christmas with me.

The holidays were a busy time for the Knicks City Dancers. I arrived early in the afternoon in my sweatpants and sneakers and rehearsed in the empty arena. We spent hours positioning ourselves into lines based on the giant Knicks logo at center court. I always stood in the back of the line, which meant no one saw me on the huge screen that hung from the roof. It also meant the players and anyone on the opposite side of the arena got a nice view of my behind for the minute and 32 seconds that we actually danced.

While we rehearsed, I tried to concentrate on my steps and style, but I had a hard time not daydreaming. In a few days, Dreamer would sit somewhere in "celebrity" row, not caring whatsoever about the basketball game. He would only care about the time-outs when I would run out with a smile and dance for him. The arena held more than 20,000 people, but there was only one person I would be thinking of as I sat in the locker room, flattening stray hairs and applying smoky eye make-up.

During our Christmas holiday, we shuttled around New York in hats and mittens. We took pictures in front of the tree at Rockefeller Center. We rode a carriage through Central Park. We went ice skating. It was such a wonderful time and it seemed unfair to the rest of the world that the two of us should have everything. We robbed the bank of happiness and kept all of it for ourselves. I knew I deserved it. I knew he did too.

Away from our families, we ate Chinese takeout on Christmas Eve and watched *The Nightmare Before Christmas* on my tiny television. On Christmas morning, Dreamer presented me with a beautiful gold locket from the 1800s. On the outside, he had it inscribed with one word: love. It was stunning. I refused to take it off my neck for the next three years. I gifted Dreamer with the book *How to Sing For Dummies*. At the time, he was so much more in love with me than I was with him. I chose to keep it light and funny, and he went right to the lovey-dovey stuff. I think he was so kind because he was never sure where he stood with me. I was so incredibly happy and told anyone but him.

A few days before New Year's, I was invited to Paris to dance at the All-Star basketball game. The entire world would be watching. A team of dancers and I flew to France, slept for two hours and arrived inside the arena. No one spoke English. Inside our locker room was sparkling water and baguettes. We ran to center court among deafening screams from the French fans and I felt higher than ever. My blood was replaced with electricity and the voltage shocked through my veins. The next morning, the dancers and I woke up early, eager not to miss out on our five available hours to see the sights of Paris. I stood underneath the grandness of the Eiffel Tower, pulled out my journal and wrote:

I'm in Paris, surrounded by the most beautiful things I have ever seen. All I can think about is you. There is not a monument on earth that can come close to matching how beautiful you are to me.

We rushed to the airport to catch our long flight back to New York beyond tired, having been awake for most of the last 76 hours. All around me, girls dressed in orange, blue and black lay fast sleep across plane seats. I applied a full set of make-up and attempted to make something acceptable out of my hair. When I walked off the plane, I was dressed in a black flapper dress and heels, with exactly 45 minutes to make it to Times Square.

That New Year's Eve, Dreamer's band played on a television special right in the middle of Times Square. As the clock hit midnight and confetti covered every square inch from 41st to 55th Street, Dreamer kissed me sweetly.

We went to the after party, and I watched the boys in the band taste their first drinks of alcohol. Their managers brought over bottle after bottle and concocted drinks like they were building castles in a sandbox. Dreamer actually drank and got very drunk. When I asked him what his New Year's resolution was, he replied, "I don't have one, I have everything I want." He leaned in and kissed me, and someone took a photo. Then, I made everyone take a family photo. His managers, his huge bodyguard and the other girlfriends all stood on the street, freezing and smiling. I had everything I wanted too.

Later on, I woke up in the middle of the night and looked over at Dreamer who was wide awake and crying. Confused, I crawled closer to him. He was watching *The Notebook* on his laptop, the scene where the lead characters were reuniting. They kissed in the rain and screamed their love for one another. "It's just so sad," Dreamer said through tears. This was the Dreamer I knew. He was so good at holding it all together for the cameras and looking dashing in his designer duds, but something deep inside him was troubled. He hid this from almost every person in his life successfully. We hear the real him in his lyrics and music, but the person presented to the world was an act. Dreamer was barely afloat for most of his ride on the famewagon.

We spent Valentine's Day in Las Vegas and decided to exchange love letters. I already knew how he felt about me because almost every minute of my day was filled with some sort of sweet message from him, but I was still so afraid to let Dreamer know how I felt. I learned from my past to keep my true feelings to myself. Men seemed to like the challenge of trying to break into my heart. But alas, Valentine's Day came and we exchanged letters. His came to me on vintage card stock, pressed with a wax seal. The words of the letter were some of the sweetest I ever heard, with statements about how he would never hurt me and how lucky he felt to be loved by me. *How he would never hurt me.*

Next I gave Dreamer my present, a handcrafted memory box with pictures of us on the outside. I wanted to write so many things to him – that I was head over heels for him, that I was scared of him, that I was still reeling over past heartbreak, that I would give up everything to spend my days with him – but I couldn't bring myself to give away that much of my heart. So instead, I put a single piece of paper inside the box with three words: I love you.

The look of disappointment on Dreamer's face when he received his letter was devastating. I felt awful. I wished I could've given him what he wanted, all of me, but I didn't have a whole me to give away. I was cautious to give away the little bit of my heart I had left.

Now, I understand why I was careful. Dreamer's sweet texts and actions melted my heart, but warning flags still shot up. One night, Dreamer accidentally pocket dialed me at 4 a.m. while I was in New York and he was at a loud party in Vegas. I listened to a 12-minute mess of words four times before I really understood what he was saying to someone else: "She's not really my girlfriend." Dreamer tried so hard to get me to love him while also trying to enjoy his life away from me.

I never should've accepted his lame excuse for that incident, or any other one after, but I knew my true feelings even if he didn't – I was in over my head. I wanted us to work out so badly that I overlooked the fact that Dreamer wasn't as innocent as he appeared. But back on that Valentine's Day evening, after disappointing him with my small note, I grabbed my computer and wrote my love letter. I told him everything I knew I shouldn't. I gave him my heart. I was completely honest, open and vulnerable. I set the letter aside for him to read when I left the next morning to fly back to New York.

Chapter 11

That summer in New York, I was a busy girl. I landed a weekly dance gig performing at The Box on the Lower East Side. I would leave my uptown apartment at 11 p.m. and take the subway downtown for my midnight call time. The show started at 1 a.m. and I came home as the sun rose each morning. I pressed play on my iPod and listened to "Midnight Show" by The Killers on the 30-minute subway ride, pretending movie cameras followed me and the song was the soundtrack to the "hard working dancer moment" montage in the movie of my life.

When I arrived at The Box, I carefully applied my make-up, watching as the girls in the cast drank wine and talked about the craziness after the show the night before. They talked about the hunky celebrities in the crowd and the hotels they went back to with them. We dressed in our tiny costumes and silk robes and were escorted up to the stage to dance. The summer air was fresh and my life was exciting, full of celebs and full of drama. Sting once sat in the front row and told me I was gorgeous. I watched celebrities enjoy their 15 minutes of fame in the VIP boxes that lined the upper level.

The only problem with this work time frame was that my daytime dance life hadn't slowed down. I would wake up before 10 a.m., heading to auditions and booking jobs after getting home at 6 a.m. and texting Dreamer goodnight. Then, 45 minutes later, I would wake up and text him good morning. I worked as an assistant choreographer on a music video for a cute rock band from the UK. The director was far more famous than the band. I had to be on set each day by 8 a.m. I lived on less than an hour of sleep, drinking constant coffee and Diet Coke, hoping that whatever breaks I made in myself were worth the breaks in the industry.

I loved being behind the scenes and in charge on the video shoot. We spent five days in the dance studio, setting the choreography. I scrambled to learn everyone's names, hovered over my notebook and attempted to appear more educated in the world of choreography than I actually was. My Type A personality was perfect for getting things done quickly on set. I would go down to make-up and check on the dancers, fit their tights when they were crooked as they walked out of wardrobe and make coffee for the choreographer. Once we started shooting, I stood off camera and did every step of choreography full out where the dancers could see me. If they got lost on a step, it would ruin the take and I wanted to help them as much as possible.

I was exhausted but thrilled. The director was far happier with me than the lead choreographer, if for no other reason than I had no backbone and ran around doing everything she asked. It's difficult for me not to work as hard as I possibly can at everything. It wasn't lost on me how long I spent hoping these opportunities would be mine. I refused to take them for granted. The band members were British and strikingly beautiful. I was quick to find a reason to bring up Dreamer and how much I loved him.

The next week, while catching up on some sleep, my agent called about an upcoming television spot with pop superstar

Fergie. I never worked with the choreographer, but she wanted a dancer who could do old school Fosse-style choreography. I auditioned in my typical "commercial" dance outfit – ballroom heels, thigh-high legwarmers, booty shorts and a bra, a black-cropped sweater and my signature scarf tied ninja-style over my forehead. All over town, people knew me as the "headband" girl. People thought I was trying to make a statement when really, I wanted to disguise my dull, broken hair. In my busy life-list of things to do, eating properly and drinking enough water always came last, and it showed with my parched strands.

Tons of girls auditioned, and some were my friends who were much better dancers than me. We danced a combination to "Glamorous," and I kept making it through round after round of cuts. Of the 12 girls the choreographer hired, only one was blonde – me! I was shocked.

A week later, I danced on national television with one of the biggest stars of the year. I let everyone know the date, time and station.

Backstage in costume, I was disappointed after checking and rechecking my phone to see I hadn't received a good luck

message from Dreamer. What the rest of the world thought
didn't matter. If he was missing from the equation, I was sad, but
I was sure he'd be watching.

I called him later that night, ecstatic after the heart-pounding
performance. When I asked him if he saw it, he responded with,
"See what?" I was heartbroken. I reminded him about the Fergie
performance earlier that night and he apologized, saying he and
his bandmates were busy working on a song.

This became the story of my entire summer. My star rose
and fell at the same time because I could never find a way to
be important enough to Dreamer. I became an afterthought.
I was on television for two and a half minutes that night and
found it impossible to believe that whatever he was doing was so
important that he couldn't afford to step away for a few minutes.

Things got worse when I started catching Dreamer in lies.
I worked hard in New York, booking new commercials and
jobs every week. I felt like I missed out on all the exciting
moments of his life. Nonetheless, I was laid back about it. I hate
confrontation. I was never one of those girls who was constantly
jealous and bossing my guy around. I let Dreamer do whatever he
wanted and never asked questions.

I only asked one thing from him. No matter what time of
night, I wanted him to call me when he got home safely. I loved
hearing his voice before I went to sleep, and I liked knowing I
was the last person he spoke with before he went to bed.

One night, Dreamer had plans to go out and see a concert
at the Palms in Las Vegas. I wished I could be there so badly.
When his nighttime phone call came, I knew something was
wrong. He was short with me, saying he was drunk, staying
at the hotel alone. In the background, I heard a man yell that
Dreamer couldn't be in there. Dreamer lied to me and was

still out partying, calling from a closet in the basement of the Palms. I never understood why he felt the need to lie. I loved fun parties as much as the next person. In retrospect, it was probably because when he finally got back to his hotel room to call me, he wasn't alone.

We started fighting a lot and whenever I got angry, Dreamer formulated a wonderfully brilliant excuse. He was a master storyteller. He once told me that he was so good at getting around things because he spent his entire life sneaking around behind his father's strict, Catholic back. Dreamer seemed innocent, but he was still capable of deceit. It was my fault for accepting lame excuses, but when the issues blew over and Dreamer and I were good, we were so good that it instantly erased all of his wrongdoings.

During a trip to Los Angeles to visit him, we fought in a friend's kitchen after I found the puppy he recently purchased alone in the bathroom without any food or water, covered in her own feces. Dreamer left for a meeting, and I stopped by to meet him at the friend's house, not knowing he wouldn't be there.

When he returned hours later with red eyes and lame excuses, I was angry. Not only for treating me like garbage, but for the puppy too. I told him weeks prior that getting a pet was a bad decision. But he wanted what he couldn't have and bought the small beagle, and somehow thought in the middle of touring the world he would have time to be a dad to this little pup.

He told me her name was Hobo, put her in my arms and introduced me as her mommy. I instantly fell in love with her and became more protective of her than I was of my own heart. At the end of the fight, I was in tears holding the shaking puppy in my hands. Dreamer turned to me and said, "I cannot fix this right now." I left, driving down the winding roads of the Hollywood

Hills to stay with a friend.

I cut my visit short by five days and returned to New York. I cried the entire flight home. There must've been something in the water of the City of Angels because something in Dreamer changed. His mind and lungs were polluted. I wasn't angry anymore, just sad for him. I knew the difficulties in dealing with pressures and protocols of showbiz life, and I never wanted him to hit rockbottom. I thought I could protect him so he would stay the sweet and sincere boy I fell in love with forever. Los Angeles had a different plan.

Chapter 12

At home, I spent days staring at my phone and mending my heart with contemporary classes at Broadway Dance Center. After some time passed, Dreamer asked if I could come to Vegas to see him and stupidly, I did. We huddled in the cocoon of being us again in his Vegas home. We opened the windows, cried into each other's arms, and listened to the soundtrack of my favorite ballet. I could hear the background melody of the "dying swan" and felt the sense of urgency beneath our lips and fingertips. We had to save this. I turned to him and said, "If you take me out to a nice dinner and ask me back, I will say yes." He did and somehow everything was OK again.

I got my Dreamer back and was determined to get my job back with the Rockettes. I doubled up my tap and ballet classes and met up with my Rockette friends to rehearse the show's choreography. Each night, I took my tap shoes down to the lobby of my apartment complex and practiced over and over again in the huge floor-to-ceiling mirror that stood beside the mailboxes.

The day of the audition, I woke up early and carefully put my hair up in a French twist. I applied my signature Rockette red lips and dressed in my lucky leotard. I took the number two train down to 50th Street and walked the rest of the way to Radio City

Music Hall with my iPod blaring, fiercely determined to get my spot back.

Just as I was about to put on my tap shoes, I checked my phone and saw a good luck message from Dreamer. It was exactly what I needed and inside that audition, I was unbelievable. My movements were accompanied by a cymbal crash and fireworks. I took my place for the tap combination on the floor, pressed my shoulders back, and smiled a glamorous smile directly at the directors, who a year ago, hadn't given me a second look. After I executed the tap combination near perfectly, I saw a director turn to another one and give a look saying, "Well, she did it." I couldn't have been more proud. Five weeks later, I received my third contract with the Radio City Rockettes.

That year, I was cast in the Nashville Rockette cast. I performed the show multiple times a day inside the famous Grand Ole Opry. The house was always packed, and my heart was just as full. Dreamer was off the road, his new record was done and being mixed, so he had time off. He spent two weeks with me inside my little hotel room. We bought a Christmas tree at Target and made home movies. Dreamer was once again my best friend. Those were the best days in our relationship. All the confusion of him being on the road was behind us, and I was finally the star. He was happy to sit in the audience and cheer me on.

Still, somewhere in the back of my mind, I remained unsure. I would wake up in the middle of the night from horrible lucid dreams where I caught Dreamer cheating on me. I wanted so badly to trust him. In my nightmares, I walked in on him with a room full of women and would wake up crying. I had these dreams while his toes touched mine as we slept.

One of my best friends in the cast became injured and hung out with Dreamer while I was away at shows. I expressed my concern to her, and one night, she asked him if he would or had ever cheated on me. He looked directly into her eyes and said, "I would never do anything to hurt Keltie. Ever." When she reported the news back to me, a wave of relief passed over me. I was acting like such a girl, letting my worst fears dictate my reality. Dreamer's fans hated me because they wanted him, and he wanted only me. I had to believe that.

One of the best parts about the tour was cast bowling night at the run-down Nashville Bowling Center. Dreamer tagged along, and we gorged ourselves on sweet tea and laughs. Everyone in my cast adored him. They told me we looked like brother and sister, and I took that as a compliment. Dreamer would lean over and whisper in my ear that I was beautiful. I would stand up, giddy with happiness, and throw the bowling ball directly into the gutter. I had love, I couldn't expect to have bowling skills too.

Bowling wasn't my strongest suit, but happiness was. I taught Dreamer some of the steps from the Rockette show, and he looked so cute in bowling shoes performing Santa moves for the cast. He won over the hearts of my cast and was now a part of my Radio City family. For a boy who didn't come from the best family situation, he was now surrounded by two loving and accepting super-fan families.

But fans and support never completely fixed Dreamer. I wished he could be a sponge for all the love I surrounded him with. He lived it and accepted it, but continued to sleep with worry streaming across his sweet face. During the day, it made me happy to see him so happy. Once again, I was only really thinking about his feelings. My own were an afterthought. I loved him so much more than I loved myself.

After the Rockette season finished, Dreamer and I decided to take our first vacation together. We went far away to the

Caribbean islands where no one could bother us. We were surrounded by sunshine, beautiful beaches and limitless fruity drinks. It was amazing to spend time with our cell phones off and without being bothered for hours. Dreamer took his guitar down to the beach each day and we stared at the ocean, talking about our dreams and goals for the next year with the strum of a million melodies in his head, floating in the breeze.

We ate our faces off. We drank our faces off. We won something like 62,000 pesos playing blackjack while we were so drunk, we couldn't stand up straight. At some point, we lost it all but we didn't care. We stumbled home arm-in-arm though the dimly lit, cobblestone pathways of the resort. When Dreamer and I were allowed to be us, without any of the pressures or distractions from the world, we were the best of everything. The best of friends. The best of crazies. The best of lovers.

While we were on vacation, Dreamer and I analyzed life and what it meant to be in the public eye. With all of his musical confidence, Dreamer was still unsure where he belonged. I told him that in order to be an idol to people, you had to be worthy of being idolized. The ones who became timeless were people like The Beatles or Bono, who regardless of their personal situations, made people believe in a cause.

Dreamer's New Year's resolution was to "be better." I encouraged him to reinvent himself with his new record into someone who had the power to change the world. I knew he was terrified. I'm sure saving the world seemed difficult when he couldn't even save himself, but from that fear came one of the most important things he ever created. It was a personal mantra and eventually a song lyric: "Reinvent love."

I suggested creating a simple t-shirt to sell at concerts with the word "reinvent" and a heart next to it. The message was something bigger than the band or the music, something with a social conscience. He loved the idea and eventually, the shirt was made. I ended up buying five of my t-shirt ideas at Hot Topic. Dreamer played me demo after demo of songs for the new album. One of them reminded me of the sound of horses. I got up and jumped around the room, showing him a ballet move meaning "the step of the horse." The song now had a name.

Dreamer created his name, his band and his career by himself and he was brilliant. But when I wasn't working on me, I spent so much time helping him that a huge part of who I was became intertwined with his work and image, and it felt like mine somehow. I was always seen as the girl holding his hand, but what about the great ideas I inspired and the conversations about every detail?

That wasn't the first time my ideas trickled down into the public. A week later, Dreamer and I were back in Vegas. He was busy working on his music and I spent days helping him move all his stuff into his new home. While cleaning out his father's old house, I came across some cool knick-knacks, among them, a set of Russian stacking dolls. I brought them to Dreamer's new house and placed them on his mantel. Hanging out that night, we started talking about music video ideas, and I brought up the dolls. They could be huge and each time you opened them, a new adventure could be found inside. Dreamer took the idea and let his mind run free. The band's next music video was made, complete with its own set of Russian dolls.

I was more than happy to help, so not getting credit didn't bother me that much. We were a team and what was mine was his. For all the times I helped Dreamer out, he watched me practice for an upcoming Broadway audition. He bought me flights to New York and back so I could attend a one-in-a-million

chance audition. He listened to me babble incessantly about all
the things I wanted to accomplish. Whenever he went away, he
brought back little tokens of love – earrings from Prague,
postcards from Amsterdam, a stuffed animal from Australia. He
wrote love song after love song for me. Things I said or did would
constantly show up in his lyrics. I was a muse for him. A mother
for him. And during the times we actually slept in the same bed,
a woman.

For a long time, I thought it was OK to put some of my goals
and dreams on hold for him, that by standing next to this person
who was adored and praised for being so great, it somehow made
me great. I felt like the things that Dreamer created were also
mine because I played such a big part in making them happen.

I was a girlfriend and a taskmaster. I kept him focused, and I
sewed his clothes and managed his calendar. I made sure someone
came to clean the house. I did his laundry, I paid his bills on time,
and I paid my bills on time but for a completely different address.
I called his family with updates and sent birthday cards when
necessary. I did this because I loved him and he needed help. I did
this because it was only after all these things were taken care of,
that Dreamer and I could snuggle up and just be "us." To sit next
to him when he had ideas on his mind was torture. Maybe it was
a melody, maybe it was a lyric or an idea for tour. Four people
were always in the room with us: Dreamer, Keltie, Dreamer's
career and Keltie's career.

Dreamer asked me to move to Las Vegas, and I declined. He
placed a ring on my finger and along with it, a million promises.
We condo shopped and he bought the one I loved. We picked out
wallpaper, drapes, bed sheets, art and countertops. He built me a
giant, floor-to-ceiling bookcase with a ladder like in *Beauty & The
Beast* because I said if he did, I would move in. He purchased a

giant bathtub with claw feet and jets because I said if he did, I would move in. It was the running joke with our good friend and interior decorator. I could get him to buy a $5,000 bathtub, but I couldn't get him to call me each night before he went to sleep.

I had to constantly remind myself that those things were in the past, and we started fresh with the New Year. It would've been easy to give it all up for him, but I was determined to stay true to myself and my career. I belonged in New York City. My agent, my connections, my friends and the subway were all there. If nothing else, I was a terrible driver. If he wanted a girlfriend, I had to commute via subway and airplane.

I spent the year doing what I did best: working all day and staying up until all hours of the night so I could be awake when it was convenient for Dreamer and I to talk. One day, I looked at my phone on the L train at 7 p.m. after a full day of rehearsals, auditions and errands, thinking I lived my entire life alone. I shared my life with an imaginary boyfriend. His name was Dreamer and he lived on a planet where people woke up at 4 p.m. and had no grasp that New York City was three hours ahead of him.

I moved into the greatest building in Manhattan in the midst of the hippest neighborhood. I just returned from Los Angeles where I choreographed John Legend's newest music video. I was a part of New York City's most treasured precision dance troupe, and my dance blog received almost 10,000 hits a week. But no matter what I did or accomplished, I had to fake self-esteem. I put it on in the morning along with my make-up. I forced myself to act strong, confident and in control. My heart and my head were constantly fighting. Sometimes my guts got involved. They couldn't agree on what I should do with my life, my career or my heart. I built too much to stand around and watch it fall apart so I did what I always did – smiled, skipped and sucked it up. I worked harder. I exhausted myself in every aspect of life, making everything work. I refused to fail. I refused to ask for help. I refused to believe that I was anything special and instead worked overtime to create a perfect image.

I headed out for my fourth Rockette season. This time, we visited a different city each night. The first ever Rockettes Arena Tour was worth millions and was the pride and joy of Radio City. In addition to the 32 Rockettes on tour, there were 45 other dancers and singers, company managers, stage managers, wardrobe managers, wig makers, athletic trainers, 150 male crewmembers, 37 semi-trucks, seven sheep and three camels. I played many of the same arenas I followed Dreamer to on his last tour. We performed to a sold-out crowd, in arenas his band could only half-fill.

Dreamer came out to visit me on tour. I happened to be on crutches after suffering nerve damage in my leg. I was out of the show for five days, and I was unsure that I would ever dance again. Seeing my body fall apart made me cling to Dreamer even more. In a random hotel room, with an ice bag on my leg, we talked about everything – the semi-flop of his latest record, the fact that magazines weren't calling anymore and the ups and downs of the tainted entertainment business. He said to me through tears, "You're the only one who really knows me and the only person who really cares about me. Everyone else is nothing." I knew it was true. Dreamer's star was falling. I loved him anyway. I loved him more, I think.

For Christmas, I decided to make Dreamer a stocking, similar to the one my mom handcrafted for me when I was a child. One thing I always remembered about helping Dreamer clean out his father's old house after his death was the lack of family memorabilia. There were a few photos, some random hockey pictures and not much else.

Dreamer's stocking looked like it was bought last minute at a drug store. I love crafts and had countless hours backstage at arenas to kill, so I started hand beading, sewing and embroidering a stocking for him in early November so it would be ready for Christmas. Every day, before I started my warm-up on tour, the girls would come over to see the progress I made on my craft project. They "oohed" and "awwed" over every new stitch, sequin and bead. I was so proud. Each addition was a stitch to put the person I loved more than anything back together. It was pathetic that I thought a good craft project could save him (or me from him). We were young and volatile show people. It was a confusion so hot, it burned my tongue every time I went in for a taste.

Chapter 13

Whenever I went on the road with Dreamer, everyone called me "his girl" instead of by my name. It wasn't just me though. All the guys, whether they were in the band or a member of the crew, always referred to their girlfriends, girls they were flirting with or girls they impressed with backstage passes for the night as "their girl."

For so long, I thought this was a term of endearment. A cool, rock 'n' roll lifestyle saying that meant I was special. I was one of a few girls in the world who could be a part of it. I was the Chuck Taylor of cute girlfriend nicknames. But I was terribly wrong. I was called that for protective purposes. Almost no one knew my name because almost no one knew I was actually Dreamer's girlfriend or that he was in a supposedly committed relationship with me. The "girl" name came from everyone around him not wanting him to get caught in a lie. It never crossed my mind that perhaps the list of girls he was walking onto the tour bus was so long that we needed to be all called by the same name to avoid confusion.

That year on my own tour, I realized that I knew the name of every one of the Rockettes' boyfriends. I knew what they did for a living, the next time they would be coming out for a visit, how they met, where they first kissed and was most likely friends with them on Facebook. I knew this because we were always talking about our guys. I spoke about Dreamer as if he sat beside me at all times. Every man on the crew knew I was taken, they knew my boyfriend's name, they knew he wore a size 10 shoe, and they knew I was head over heels for him. I made it impossibly clear so no lines could ever be blurred.

Whenever I walked into a room, none of Dreamer's friends looked me in the eye. I knew his bandmates were thrown into the spotlight just as their own self-image was being built, so they preferred interaction between the four of them, give or take a manager or a bodyguard, than interaction with the rest of the world. I chalked their hung heads up to their adolescent awkwardness.

During the Rockette arena tour, I received an e-mail from the editors of *Dance Spirit* magazine completely out of the blue. I was in shock as I read the e-mail and learned they were interested in having me as the cover girl for their April issue. I screamed, jumped around the room and called Dreamer right away. He didn't answer, which was something I was used to, so I left a voicemail. If he answered, I would've explained that *Dance Spirit* was basically the *Rolling Stone* of dance and anyone who was anyone was on the cover.

The editors were interested in me because they were publishing the dance team issue, and I had danced for the Knicks, the Nets and the Rockettes. I worked so hard for so many years that the magazine wanting me for any reason other than because I was a great dancer, was lost on me. I was amazed at how many mean girls said I got that cover because of Dreamer. He may have helped bring my name out a little bit, but the successes the article credited me with all happened before I dated him.

Trickle down fame was strange. I liked to think that my newfound media success was the natural progression after years of cutthroat work, but I also had to realize that everyone loved a good story. The romance between a Rockette and a rockstar who met onstage at an awards show at Radio City Music Hall was an easy one to sell. After all, I certainly thought it was the most romantic thing ever, serendipitous of both sides of my heart and life. There were huge cracks, in me, in my career, and in my relationship with Dreamer, but to anyone watching, I was the stuff dreams were made of.

The day before my cover shoot, I had tea with a good friend in New York. She was upset to hear that Dreamer hadn't driven me to the airport in Las Vegas to wish me luck on the biggest photo shoot of my life. She spoke about all the things I deserved and how she thought Dreamer was falling short on giving any of them to me. My friend encouraged me to ask for what I deserved and said I was wasting my time if I wasn't getting it. She couldn't care less who he was or what he did and was far more concerned with what he was to me. It was difficult for me to explain our magic when it was just the two of us. I blamed distance for getting in the way.

But how could I be mad when the reason Dreamer was so tired the morning of my flight was because he just flew back from a trip with his band? I could take the distance because brilliant things about how much he loved me would come out of his mouth. I would wake up to an e-mail saying things like, "I wrote a song for you… *If I could ask for anything I'd only want my girl…*"

That day, I was in a studio downtown and everyone in the room gushed over the shoot. The girls and editors fawned over me, saying they would totally hate me if I wasn't so sweet. They told me I was perfect. Despite my insecurities and all the times I fell flat on my face, I felt special that day. I didn't need to pretend or plan, I was just Keltie.

During one of our breaks, the editor and I sat down for a cup of tea and went over a few extra questions for my interview. I asked her what Dreamer said about me when she interviewed him, and she banned me from looking at the paper. She said, "I can't tell you what he said, but I can tell you that everyone in the office wishes he was our boyfriend." I was never more proud. All the things my friend and I agonized over the day before were erased. Dreamer was once again redeemed.

My only regret is how much I talked about Dreamer in the interview. I spoke of my love for him and how much I appreciated his support and how special our relationship was. I wish I was a little more self-centered and a little less us-centered. I didn't care at the time because I wasn't expecting to be lying in bed crying my eyes out on the morning my *Dance Spirit* issue arrived in the mail, staring at a cover which featured a headline about me and my ex-boyfriend. The interview and photos were still amazing. Dreamer said some pretty wonderful things that will always stay with me. He said I made him want to be a better person. It felt like the greatest compliment I could've ever received.

The next week was a much-needed vacation. Dreamer and I chose a Hawaiian resort far away from the rest of the world. I was two weeks away from starting a new dance contract in Las Vegas for Jerry Mitchell's show, *Peepshow*, which I workshopped years before in New York City, when we first met. I was in the middle of moving in with Dreamer and buying a car, and I needed a break from the almost seven straight months of work I was doing. I was finally ahead in my bank account and in my career. I definitely looked forward to being lazy for a few days in the sun.

The trip was incredible. We had the best time swimming with dolphins, watching huge turtles lay on the sandy beach, and taking our nightly walks to the hot tub. It was one of the best weeks of my life and I didn't see a single sign of the impending doom on its way. Dreamer stared at me directly in the eyes and told me how much he loved me, which seemed so heartfelt. I believed him. I believed that each year we got a little older and a little more of the growing pains of our lives together sorted themselves out. I believed we would be together forever.

The night of Valentine's Day, Dreamer drove up from Los Angeles to spend the night with me. I moved all my stuff into his Vegas pad as I prepared to start my new job in a few days. Finally, after all our time apart, we were living together! He walked in the door with a giant flower arrangement and hugs and kisses for me. We got dressed up and he took me to a sold-out Billy Joel concert at the MGM.

We sat in the fifth row and held hands as we sung along to all the great tunes. When Billy played "She's Got a Way," Dreamer held me close and whispered in my ear that the song was written for me. I blushed. That night on the way back to the car, we ran into one of his bandmates' parents and talked on the street for a bit. I was amazed at the family we created through the intertwining of both of our worlds.

Worried that we would have to stand in line for hours at valet, Dreamer grabbed my hand and we ran giggling past all the 40-somethings at the concert, like kids in a schoolyard. We were both terrible runners and threatened to trip at any moment, but somehow we made it home that night, back into each other's arms and back into bed. It was a perfect Valentine's Day, one of the few we were actually able to spend together. We lay in bed that night, talking about how finally, everything worked out. We were both in the same city, working and happy with our sleeping dog between us. Perfection reached us and it was an unbelievable feeling.

Chapter 14

The next morning I woke up early to make Dreamer breakfast. I crept downstairs and started cooking pancakes and bacon. I must've really loved him because I was cooking meat for him! The beautiful Valentine's Day flowers sat on the table beside me.

Dreamer's phone lit up on the counter, and I went over to see if it was anything important, like a call from his manager or bandmates. A text message window popped up from a girl whose name I didn't recognize. I think the text said, "Happy Valentine's Day, baby. xoxoxo." I can't remember for sure because the next thing I knew, I started throwing up in the sink. I felt completely dumbfounded. Was it a wrong number? It couldn't be. How else would her name be programmed in his phone?

I never looked through anyone's phone before. After all the things Dreamer and I went through, I never felt the need to look. The day after Valentine's Day, I cooked meat for the man I loved, without knowing he was seeing someone on the side, going to her house and sending late-night messages for weeks. My face flushed as I scrolled through the messages.

I honestly can't and don't want to remember what I saw that day, but the dates registered with me. I saw the date of my birthday two weeks before, the day I received two huge bundles

of flowers while spending some time with my family in Canada.
He was with her on my birthday. I scrolled back farther and
realized he texted her while we were on vacation in Hawaii. He
sang me love songs on the beach while also thinking about some
girl.

Some of the messages were about her getting off work. It
seemed she was a waitress. My whole adult life I struggled to stay
afloat and have an awesome career so I would never have to be a
dancer/waitress and here he was, more interested in her. I was
successful. I was in commercials, print advertisements, movies
and music videos. None of it was enough. For him, this waitress,
this random girl, was worth ruining everything.

I was red, hot and ill. I ran upstairs and threw the phone at
his sleeping head. I went to the closet, grabbed a bag and started
packing a few necessities. He woke up and asked, "Baby, what are
you doing?" I turned and said, "Do not look at me. Do not speak
to me. You disgust me."

I bawled my eyes out and he stood there in shock. He didn't
speak. He didn't try to explain. I packed my things and got
dressed, grabbed my car keys and our dog. I stood at the bottom
of the stairs and looked up at him with tears in my eyes, asking,
"Do you have anything to say for yourself?"

He stuttered and started to say, "She's nothing. She means
nothing to me." I slammed the door before he could finish
talking.

I left even though I had nowhere to go. I pulled over on the
side of the road and gasped for air in between open-mouthed
sobs. For a few minutes afterward, I felt like I played a part in the
greatest break-up movie of all time and none of it was real. At
any moment, the director would yell "cut" and I would be back
making pancakes, living in my perfect world with my post-

Valentine's Day glow.

Catching Dreamer cheating was devastating. My emotions were a mix of wanting to throw away all my values and tell him it was OK, then feeling pure hatred. I went through a rollercoaster of emotions. I remembered every special occasion and wondered if he was cheating on me at that time too. The band guy who messes around was such a cliché. Something special set him apart from the rest. I was sad that it was gone.

The memories of our almost three years together played over and over in my head. I felt like he stole those years from me.

I tried to be strong, but I was a pathetic mess. Minutes felt like hours, and I tried not to throw up. I wanted to believe in everything he was. I wanted to believe I was so important to him that he would be sitting in Los Angeles, meditating and writing in his journal about how he was going to sort out his adolescent mind, drive up to Las Vegas and beg me to come back. He always wore the Buddhist meditation beads I brought him back from China, but never actually meditated. Maybe he started, but then again, maybe I was just a fool and he was just a liar. The feeling of nauseating reality set in when I realized nothing changed for Dreamer, except he was free to do whatever he wanted, without having to text message me good night before seeing someone else.

Someone once told me that the history of rock music is littered with bodies of incredibly talented people who thought they could deal with the alcohol, drugs and everything else the lifestyle offered without it changing them. The person I met in 2006, the one who despised everything about the music industry, let it eat him alive, and now, even though I was initially cautious about giving my heart to him, I was eaten alive as well. I could barely breathe. He moved to the dark side, and I was left mourning the death of our love and the death of the person I was so madly in love with. This man didn't exist anymore, if he ever did at all, and he never would again.

I wore black and stopped eating. I thought about calling him, and realized that he most likely was happy to get caught. Dreamer had a way of dislodging everyone from his life when they got too close. If you started to know his secrets and knew he wasn't as perfect, innocent or ideal as his public persona made him out to be, he slowly pushed you out of his life and moved onto someone else to start fresh with.

I never questioned his choice of friends until I started listing the reasons why it was better we were over in my journal. I realized they included a girl who hit on a married man while he sat beside his very pregnant wife backstage at the House of Blues, a guy who had pockets full of powder and a bunch of people who called me "his girl" for years. These weren't the type of people I wanted to be around.

When I called my brother to tell him the news, he acted like I just told him that peanut butter goes with jelly. Of course he told you he was different. Of course he was a loser in high school. Of course he cheated on you now that he was famous. If men are only as faithful as their options, Dreamer was like a kid in a candy store. A candy store full of pretty blondes, jumping at the chance to be with someone who was famous. It didn't matter that to most people above the age of 17, Dreamer was as exciting as wallpaper. He had a name and a claim to fame, thus he was lusted after for all the wrong reasons.

Learning to live alone again was impossibly heartbreaking. My nights were restless and I woke up exhausted from dreaming of him. I recounted his imperfections over and over, and still longed to feel his soft skin next to mine. I knew I deserved more, but I couldn't help it. It's pathetic what women are willing to sacrifice for love. It's a disturbing wake-up call when you spend every day thinking about and being with someone, and the day arrives when you can't do that anymore. You know the person you love is still out there, but you have to pretend that he's dead.

When I woke up the morning after I left, the burning in my chest was so terrible, I thought I might've had a 105-degree fever. I felt nauseous. I still thought there was a way for us to get back together, perhaps it was just a bad fight. Every time I heard a noise, I thought it might be him showing up at the doorway with flowers, begging me to take him back. Every time I heard the phone ring, I was sure he called to apologize and make everything better. Instead, the calls were from wonderful friends who listened to me cry for hours and said things like, "You are so much better off without him. He didn't deserve you. You will be OK." The idea of actually being "OK" was so far off. I felt like I might never shower again, let alone be OK. I called every single person in my phone because I couldn't stand to be alone with my heart.

On the second day, I woke up crying. It felt like someone ripped out my insides and replaced them with fire. I was sure that today he would come crawling back. I went to move all my stuff out of his house and sobbed to a neighbor who I only met once before.

The next day, I woke up and didn't cry. Somehow, my heart started to cool, and the pain and burning rested in my stomach. I realized that I hadn't eaten or brushed my teeth in three days. There was a twinkle of hope that one day I might be all right. My friends started to give me the "strong" talk. The one that goes, "You're so strong and you need to be with someone who really cares about you." It was hard to hear because for all the time I was with Dreamer, I thought he cared about me. I felt so stupid for believing and making excuses for him.

On the fourth day, I took a shower – a short one. The act of standing alone in a bathtub without someone to support or comfort me was almost impossible. It took all of the courage in my body to keep from crying every time I took a breath. I was so thin, a friend practically had to force-feed me. I wrote an e-mail with all of the nasty things I wanted to say to him and almost hit send. I hadn't cried, and I was already awake for almost 45 minutes. I wanted to go back to sleep and wake up months later when my heart didn't hurt so badly.

By day five, I ate two meals. I thought about him all the time, but tried to be positive. I sent him the e-mail, not sure if he would respond, and not sure if I actually wanted him to. I missed him, but I had a small feeling that my life might be better without him. I couldn't believe I was thinking that so soon.

The days passed, and I started waking up feeling OK. He responded to my e-mail and said he wasn't fighting for me because I deserved better. I hate that line. I heard it in two songs and most romance films. I felt so abandoned. It would've been easier if he was fighting for me. I got the, "it's not you, it's me" line. The cliché didn't keep me from feeling like everything was wrong with me. He also told me that I was too good for him and a better person than he was. Most likely, that was the only truth he ever spoke to me. He told me he felt like a horrible person. He was wrong, he *was* a horrible person.

After work, I cried on the entire drive home. Sometimes I woke up and felt mad. I was determined to get over him, but it was hard not to try to make everyone in the world hate him too. I tried my best to be classy, to be the bigger person, but he didn't deserve classy. I tried not to use the word "hate," even though it poured out of my heart. After the shock set in, I wanted nothing more than to put him in front of a line of Rockettes and let them high kick him in the face, one by one.

A week after I left, I thought, "One week ago my life was perfect. We were dancing to 'She's Got a Way' and he held me closer than ever." I hated how slowly time passed. I prepared for the second wave of heartache. I wished so badly that he would write me to see if I was OK. I tried to go out each night and meet new people, but it just made me depressed, and I would wander home to the comfort of my bed and snuggle with our dog.

Despite Dreamer's peculiarities, I always felt special being with him and was proud to be his. Now, I just blended into the background. My self-confidence was shot and I was convinced that I was doomed to be alone forever.

I kept almost nothing involving Dreamer around after that. It made me sick to see those things. I transferred every video and picture of us onto a hard drive and hid it at the bottom of a box. I covered the painting he made for me with tissue paper. I threw all of his band's memorabilia into the box too. I packed every card, flower, picture frame and ticket stub. I left everything he ever gave me on the kitchen table at his apartment.

I maliciously wished that it would knock out his soul when he came home – the same way the truth about him knocked out my heart. I thought if I could remind him of all the things we did and the kind words he said to me, the numerous times he said he loved me, that somehow it would shock him into still loving me. Of course, Dreamer left me many months before I caught him. He was out of our relationship and moved on before I even knew it was over. Our years left lying on the table wouldn't affect him now. It would turn into more garbage unattended in the trashcan that was emptied only by maids or me. I'm sure our entire collection of memories was discarded without thought, much like I was.

I took only one thing: the first love letter he wrote me, still sealed with wax, like in the movies he loved so much. It was in that letter that he vowed to never hurt me, where he told me how lucky he felt to be loved by me and in it, promised me the world.

One of the girls in my new show suggested I go to therapy. She was dragged through the mud in a similar fashion the year before and credited having outside help to the excellent condition of her heart. So, I went to therapy.

The first time I went to therapy was the first time I was ever completely honest. I actually had to give myself a pep talk about being honest on the way over. It wouldn't help if I didn't tell the truth.

My truth was horrible, and I hated what I was. I was the girl who existed solely for a guy. When the therapist told me she thought I was co-dependent and gave me some paperwork on it, a light bulb went off inside my head. I was never alone, and losing Dreamer was more than losing Dreamer, it was being alone, which was the most terrifying thing ever.

I was co-dependent. Duh. It was so nice to finally have a name for it. My constant need to please others, my ability to make anything work, even if it was awful, just so I didn't have to be alone. I had a disease in my heart. I needed a cure. Unfortunately, they don't make a magic pill for heartache.

I was determined not to make a fool of myself during this break-up, but I knew it was impossible. One of my favorite comedians had a skit about a girl who makes numerous excuses to see her ex. She needs her CDs back, she needs her sweater, just so she could talk to him again. I wanted to talk to Dreamer and tell him how much I missed him and that if he ever needed me, I would be around. I wanted to tell him to come back, to kiss me and make this better. In my head, this seemed less pathetic than asking for my CDs back, but it wasn't. Not by a long shot.

Having a broken heart messed with my mind in ways I didn't think were possible. I would wake up in the morning feeling strong and by the time I went to sleep, was on the verge of calling him or getting in my car and driving to Los Angeles. I wondered just how badly someone could treat me before I took the hint.

My therapist gave me homework. I had to make a list of all the expectations I have for the way others treat me. Some of the things on my list were:

Do what you say you are going to do.
Be honest.
Be happy for me when good things happen.
Be nice to me.

My therapist told me that my expectations were pretty pathetic. Those are things all humans should do. She said I needed to set the expectation bar higher and that hit home with me. I never gave myself a break. The standards I held for myself were way higher than what I expected from anyone else. This was a good lesson. I became accustomed to being used, talked down to, cut at auditions and treated badly, that somehow it morphed into acceptable behavior in my real life. I had a hard time separating the two lives I had.

The day after therapy, I woke up happy. Happy that I knew what was wrong with me and was determined to beat it. By nighttime, I was sad and lonely again. I thought maybe Dreamer also wanted to become a better person and that we could get better together. I wanted to fix myself but at the same time, I still wanted to fix him.

Problem was, he didn't want to be fixed. I knew I had to cut off all contact, but I couldn't help it. I was so excited to tell him about what I learned in therapy, about us being twin co-dependents, and I asked him to call me sometime between 6 p.m. and midnight. By 10:30, I gave up on the idea that he would ever call. Once again, he disappointed me.

I still missed him. I was so sad. I couldn't believe that after so many positive breakthroughs, I was back to feeling sad. I hoped I was moving on to acceptance. I wanted to pass Go. I wanted to collect $200. I wanted my heart back.

I tried too hard to conceal my sadness. I woke up every morning and attended long rehearsal days for my show. It was the talk of the town and I was lucky to have this job, especially now. I went to a work environment each day where I was constantly being told how amazing and gorgeous I was. I used my talent each day and was able to watch in the mirror as I perfected the role. I was surrounded by the best of friends, all of whom had the best advice to give. Nothing helped, and every day when my work ended, I cried all the way home in my car, unsure if I could gather the strength and courage to do it all again tomorrow. Somehow, I did. I pushed myself to the extreme, both emotionally and physically.

One night I got a text from Dreamer at 3 a.m. I felt happy that he was lonely. I felt beautiful and strong at rehearsals and then came home, heard a song and felt my heart breaking again. Pieces of my heart scattered all over the carpet in my rented room. Hobo would get up, sniff around and look up at me as if to say, "We should put this back together now." I did everything I could not to call. I wondered if he would call me. I still thought maybe we could work it out. I was that stupid. I wished I scheduled more therapy appointments because I felt like I might go mad before my next one on Monday. Small parts of me knew I was better off now, but they were so miniscule that they blended in with all the hurt and sadness. I begged time to pass faster.

A month later, I woke up in a hospital bed after passing out at work on the bathroom floor at rehearsals. I was on what's commonly known as the "break-up diet" of Diet Coke, coffee and not much else. Getting out of bed, making dinner or having the energy to lift a fork to my mouth was impossible. There's a great Ani DiFranco lyric that says, "Did I ever tell you that I stopped eating when you stopped calling me?" That couldn't have been truer for me. I'm hypoglycemic, and my break-up diet mixed with my body's low tolerance to sugar levels was enough to put myself into sugar shock. I passed out and my body was only a few sugar levels away from shutting down into a coma. For all the things I loved and lost in life, this was my absolute rockbottom. In rehearsal, I fell to the floor with castmates and stage managers whizzing around me. My body wouldn't let me get up. My brain kept thinking, "I just want to lie here on this cold floor, and go to sleep for a very long time."

Hooked up to IVs and half asleep, I begged my roommate to call Dreamer. I wanted him to know I was sick. I wanted him to feel scared that he might lose me, as if that could jolt his heart into caring enough to change his ways. It would be the perfect chance for him to hop on his white horse with his suit of armor and carry me off into the sunset. It was a terrible idea and one more chance for him to disappoint me. I had no reason to feel that he might suddenly become compassionate or that me being a mess would help him realize I was something he couldn't live without. I was in awe of my stupidity for thinking otherwise. I was so stupid to think I still mattered to him.

Walking back into rehearsals and having to look at the pity in my coworkers' eyes was embarrassing. I found out later that some ruthless cast members made fun of me and fake fainted around the hallways. I was too exhausted to care. No one could understand the shock of losing your house, lover and best friend unexpectedly. Feeling that betrayal, I started to question everything I ever believed in. I was lucky I only fainted because driving my car into oncoming traffic had, at times, seemed like a good idea.

I alienated myself from almost everyone in the show and found myself eating lunch alone in the seats of the theater. I stared at the huge, beautifully lit sign and thought about how years prior, when I first started dating Dreamer and was in workshops for this very show, one of my friends warned me to stay away, that rockstars were bad news. I vented to another friend that it was awful for anyone to say that about Dreamer because he was different. But rockstar stereotypes aren't manufactured out of nowhere. I loved and lost enough men of the music variety to be a testament to this rule.

Every day at lunch, I carbo-loaded, hoping to gain weight fast before opening night so I could keep my job. The director, Jerry Mitchell, sat down next to me one day. In the middle of putting together a $12 million show, he came to talk to me when lights should be checked, automation cues should be set and costumes should be approved.

Jerry told me that when he was 31 years old, he broke up with his boyfriend of seven years and thought he would die. He believed this was the person he would spend the rest of his life with. He described the pain of the break-up and how he used the passion of the pain to focus on work. He spent the next year joining *The Will Rogers Follies* and getting into amazing shape. As a way of building up his self-esteem again, he created the first *Broadway Bares*, a benefit for Broadway Cares/Equity Fights AIDS. During the next 19 years, the popularity of *Broadway Bares* led to *Peepshow*. It etched Jerry's name as one of the most sought after directors on Broadway and in Hollywood.

It took him 10 years to ever really trust anyone again. "Ten years," I thought. "I'm 27 years old. In 10 years, I'll be 37 and not wasting any trust on young boys, I hope."

Jerry cheered me up by telling me how amazing I was in his show and how glad he was that I came to Vegas to open his dream show with him. He reassured me that everything would be OK and that I was never meant to be some guy's "girl" because I stand too tall on my own. He instructed me to look at the stage, take it all in and know that dancing is what really matters. The stage isn't leaving.

I told him how well I was doing and even though I was hurting, I was healing. I told him what I started focusing on – me. I told him that I didn't want to be like every other dancer and that I wanted more – an empire, a name, to be Jerry one day. He said I could have it all because anything is possible.

I held back tears and instructed myself, "Do not cry in front of Jerry. Do not cry in front of Jerry. This man cast you as a sex symbol. This man is casting *Catch Me if You Can* on Broadway next season. This man is gay and knows you should've picked waterproof mascara this morning."

I've never seen Jerry upset. I've never seen him not smiling. I've never seen him not in awe of the world. I see so much of myself in him and I'm so thankful he shared his story with me. Life is such an adventure and if someone told me five years prior that I'd be having a heart-to-heart with a Tony Award winner like Jerry, I never would've believed it.

Jerry went back to work, and I watched him plan the show's lighting. I watched our spicy star play with her adorable 2-year-old daughter and became filled with faith. For a brief moment, I felt like I was going to be OK. But as soon as I finished my rice and beans and found myself back in the hallways beneath the stage, I remembered just how alone I really was.

Chapter 15

I saw Dreamer at the dog park once. He looked frail. I expected him to say that hurting me was the biggest mistake of his life and that he would do anything to get me back. He didn't of course, and in one of my more pathetic moments I said, "I don't believe that you do not want to kiss me." He said it would make things complicated.

He cried and I believed they were tears of "I miss you" and "I messed up." Really, they were tears of, "I'm scared for myself," and "I'm scared for my future." Everything was always about him and he was as inconsiderate as ever. He even said, "I don't want to date you, but I don't want you to date anyone else."

I somehow found the courage to tell him not to contact me. I told him I was going to get over him and that I needed him to leave me alone. It was the strongest I was in weeks. I hoped that I would continue on this mission of strength and independence but as soon as I left, the resilience poured out of me. On the way home, I had to pull over, blinded by the tears in my eyes. Hobo sat next to me, giving me the identical look that her father gave me moments before.

Dreamer once told me, "I'm just reflecting your perfections." Maybe all of us are just mirrors to each other. I guess it's human nature to see ourselves in worse light than we actually exist in. It's like our brains are walking around in the unfortunate fluorescent lighting in office buildings when really, we exist in that enchanting light at dusk that makes everything look beautiful. Maybe perfection is in the eye of the beholder. Maybe the only two perfect things in the universe are peanut butter and La Mer face cream. Maybe we're lucky if we can see that nearly perfect is enough. Maybe we can all be perfect, just not all at the same time.

I went full force into my life and erased Dreamer's number from my phone, along with all of our mutual friends. I went through entire days without thinking of him. I loved the attention I received from the show, the press and all the fun events. I spent my days by the pool with my girlfriends and my nights drinking wine at the local hangouts in Las Vegas. One day, one of the headliners from our show told me that it was my time to shine. She said the only thing that mattered was how I treated myself and that I couldn't do anything about the way he treated me.

I spent a lot of time dancing in the studio, taking the dog for walks and writing. I wrapped my loneliness around myself like a warm, snuggly blanket. I wanted to be alone. I wanted to work on myself. I wanted to make sure that no matter what happened next or what life threw at me, that I would never put myself in a situation where I would have to feel so much pain. I was determined to get over my addiction to emotionally unavailable men in skinny jeans.

I walked out of work and gazed at the beautiful desert sky and full moon. At the show that night, some set pieces broke in the middle of one of our numbers, leaving 12 dancers on stage without our sets to swing, contort or do ballet on. Right before we walked onstage, we all looked at each other with fear in our eyes and agreed to just freestyle. I danced my way to the end of the runway. I couldn't see what anyone behind me did and for two minutes, and pulled out all of my tricks: kicks, leg hold turns and needles. I was a full out competition jazz dancer. When I turned to see what the girls did, I realized all of them just posed, looking hot and slinking around the stage.

I got off stage and my dance captain came up to me and exclaimed, "You let me have it!" I felt silly, but at the same time I felt free. In life, you have to go for it, at all times. The people around me, behind me and beside me may have been happy slinking through life, but I believed it was much better to give all of yourself to each and everything you're going to do. One hundred percent at all times. People said I was trying too hard, working too hard and loving too hard, but to me, this was a strength. I gave everything I had to whatever I did – dancing on stage, dancing in my bedroom, listening to a friend, being a friend, falling in love or falling out of love. Sometimes I ended up passed out on the floor, but other times, I felt so energized by the amazing dream life I led.

That night, I lay on my couch and had an amazing conversation with one of my friends until 7 a.m. For the first time in a long time, something made sense. My friend told me that I was really good on the inside and really good on the outside.

I wasn't always good on the inside. I could lie. I have. I could hurt. I have. I could take someone for granted in the exact way I was taken for granted. When you're beneath these levels of hurt, you're the victim and it's all you think about. When you're on the other side, when you're the one doing the hurting, you can rationalize your hurtful actions. It seemed so backwards that being the bad guy was easier than being the good guy.

I knew what it must've felt like for Dreamer to have the best standing right in front of him and not be able to realize it. To know that I would never hurt him, never leave him, never put anything above him and how badly he must have wanted to feel it. How much he wanted to feel that it was the right thing, to play along as if he could trick his heart into being smart and wanting only my goodness. I know what it must've felt like to really care about me so much, want only the best for me, and yet in the back of his head know there was no possible way it was going to be forever. I wonder what it is about people that we can never pick the best choice for us. I wonder why apologies always come long after they are actually wanted. I wonder what it is about me that says, "Treat me badly and in a few years, come back and tell me how awesome I am."

My friend and I talked about humans just being animals with a God complex. It made me so sad. I wanted to think that life was all magic, myths and movie soundtracks. Perhaps it wasn't though and we were all animals, just trying to survive.

A few months later I sent Dreamer a message telling him I was ready to be friends. I created a dream life in Las Vegas and had so many good things on my plate. I wanted him to be in my life, in whatever capacity I could have him. I invited him to see my show and gave the performance of my life. I was beautiful and confident, dancing with everything I had.

I invited him back to my place for tea after the show. He felt like home, and I wanted to hug and kiss him again. Instead, I told him to sit down, relax and let me know what was going on in his life. Out of the blue, he told me he wasn't seeing anyone, even though people e-mailed me pictures of him with a Keltie look-alike I tried to forget. After almost three years of ruthless lies, I thought that time apart maybe saved his broken soul and we were ready to become friends in honesty. But he was lying.

The next night, I went out for dinner with a good friend who was also the athletic trainer for the Rockettes arena tour. She

watched me spend hours hand sewing the stocking I made for
Dreamer. She listened to me talk about him, saw me obsess over
him and knew that I was completely in love with him.

With tears in her eyes, she told me about seeing Dreamer the
night before he saw me at Cirque du Soleil's *Love*, which is based
on music from The Beatles. Her fiancé was a cast member and
walked up to Dreamer after the show, mistaking his Keltie
look-alike date for me. Her fiancé ran up and hugged the girl
from behind, exclaiming, "HI KELTIEEE!" Dreamer's date turned
around and said, "I'm not Keltie." Dreamer took his new girl to
Love.

My heart broke. We lived and breathed that show. We made
out to its soundtrack on his record player all summer. I planned a
huge birthday party for him and his best friend and brought 25 of
his friends to see *Love* with us. I auditioned for the show because I
thought it would make him love me more. We fell in love with
each other and The Beatles simultaneously. He bought me the
entire Beatles collection on vinyl and when the huge box arrived,
we "oohed" and "ahhed" over each carefully wrapped gem. I
proudly took him to Strawberry Fields and the Lennon memorial
in New York City and we sat on the "Imagine" mosaic, holding
each other and doing our best John and Yoko peace signs, as a
tourist took our picture.

I was so easily replaced. Hot blonde women are a dime a
dozen, but there are a few with something more inside their eyes
and hearts. This new girl walked into his empty arms and picked
up where I left off. Yesterday, he sat on the couch of my new
house, telling me how he missed me and couldn't get over me.
Dreamer didn't need love, he wanted a girl in close range so he
was never lonely. A girl who didn't have a career that took her
away all the time, a girl who wanted to give up everything to be

with him. Love for him was secondary to having someone to hold at night. Hearing a Beatles song on the radio that night made me cry all over again. He ruined my heart, my *Dance Spirit* cover and now he ruined The Beatles for me.

That night, through tears, I wrote in my journal:

I have all the power. I really do. You told me you missed me and that you didn't have a girlfriend. If she meant anything to you, or was the love of your life then you might have said that and you also would have never talked to me at all. The fact that you try to keep me in your life shows that you miss me, and want to know what is going on with me, and all I need to do now is prove to you that I don't care and blow you off and throw my greatness in your face all the time.

I think it's funny how my answer to everything was to be greater than everyone. As if doing great things would make it all better. Someone asked me once where I got all of my motivation. Sadly and honestly, a lot of it comes from wanting to throw my success in the faces of the people who were mean to me. What a terrible thing to admit.

I sat back quietly and watched Dreamer's life fall apart. He told me he was doing great, but I saw the exact opposite happening. He left his band and photos of him surrounded by drugs leaked onto the Internet. His family reached out to me for help. Acquaintances said they hated the person Dreamer was turning into.

I couldn't help Dreamer because I had to help myself. It took all of my strength to not hate him. It took all of my courage to continue to be a kind and selfless person. I contacted Dreamer after the photos leaked, asking if he was OK and saying if he ever needed me, I would be there for him. He responded with, "Better than ever. Thanks for reaching out." His words weren't a response given to someone who he loved, shared everything with and just a few weeks prior had said was the only person who mattered.

Once again, he disappointed me. I took out a calendar and on each day, wrote one thing that was awful about him. Every day I went without speaking to him, I crossed out and counted as a little victory. Over time, I didn't have to remind myself that I was better off without him. I lived my life knowing that it was true.

He came back a few months later and said everything I always longed to hear. That I was irreplaceable, that he missed me, that I was the best thing that ever happened to him, that he really messed things up. I had no idea if he was telling the truth. I nodded my head and let it be. I was done fighting for Dreamer.

I wrote in my journal that night:

I will always miss you. I will always know that I'm better off without you.

Chapter 16

If anyone asked me the morning after Valentine's Day if I would ever smile, laugh or love again, I would've said no. I would've never believed it was possible. Maybe it isn't possible for me to love again. Maybe we only get a few great loves in our lives and I used mine all up. I'm not ready to find out. But I'm smiling and I'm laughing. I'm focusing on only me and finding out what it is that I really want.

Maybe my heart is like my first apartment in Queens, where I had to walk up three flights of stairs and sleep in a tiny bed, staring at the ceiling and watching the paint peel off the walls. Maybe it will never completely heal. Maybe I'll have to buy some spackle to fill in the cracks, paint over the old wall and in a few years, when the cracks start to show through, I'll have to do it all over again. I don't mind. I think I like the cracks. Life is a series of little squares of time. Life was great then, life is great now. I'm excited for the next amazing little square of time and this fresh coat of paint.

You get things back with time. For me, it was the ability to love myself. To believe in the power of love and the idea that maybe, it could happen for me again. It was the ability to look into our dog's eyes and not see Dreamer's staring back at me. The ability to wear the clothes he bought me and not feel sad, to speak about our relationship without having tears well up in my eyes. It was the ability to be happy for my friends when they fell in love and left me sitting at the singles/kids table at their weddings. It was the ability to discuss things like jeans, books and Burma without the mention of the condition of my heart.

There are some things you never get back. I still have an undying sense of the loss of my innocence. I will never get back the feeling of reckless abandon when I fell in love for the first time. I will always question other people's motives. I lost much of my ability to trust others. When people are nice to me, I instantly push them away for fear of them getting close to me. A large part of me is still mad at the world for allowing people to be lonely.

I watch people buzz around me like bees, all with the ability to connect to something. I feel disconnected to so much of the world. Everything I'm connected to is Keltie-made, so I exist in my own little bubble. If I choose not to reach out to the world for a few days, I'm never surprised to not be contacted. I sometimes feel like I fly by without showing up on anyone's radar. I think about how nice it must be to wake up somewhere and belong, knowing that the situation is forever and that the love you share isn't a trend or something that will be replaced and forgotten. I wonder what it's like to know you will never be an afterthought.

I'm sorry that any of my rockbottoms ever happened, and I'm sorry for being far crueler to myself than anyone else could. At the same time, I'm happy to know what love and success feel like. I'm happy to know what it feels like to have all of my childhood dreams come true.

Only a handful of people living in this world get to experience the life their 9-year-old selves dreamed of. If I knew then that I wasn't destined to grow up and navigate my way through love like a princess in a Disney movie, life probably would've been a little easier for me.

I still can't listen to my favorite band The Beatles without thinking of Dreamer. Too much of our relationship happened with the backdrop of these songs that I can't hear one without being able to smell him standing next to me or picturing his slender hands learning to play "Let It Be" on the piano while I drank tea and read beside him. Despite the battles going on inside him at the time, the love I felt inside of me was substantial and true. Regardless of how strong of a person you are, getting over someone, someone you loved dearly, takes time, patience and a lot of love from yourself.

I don't miss Dreamer anymore, but I sure do miss the Beatles.

Epilogue

When I left home at 18, I wanted to be a dancer. I'm happy to report I succeeded. I also had a clear picture of what my match would look like, and on that end, I haven't been as successful.

My dad once said to me, "Baby girl, you can have it all, but you can't have it all at the same time." So true. I haven't found my white picket fence. But I like to think that my time spent in the midst of my rock 'n' dance life meant something. Sometimes I look back and this story is more like a story I read and not something I actually lived. I can look at pictures and not even recognize myself. I don't feel like that girl, and maybe that's why we live through things. We hurt, we heal and we prove to ourselves that we can survive. Even more, we can rise from the adversity that life throws at us. I happened to do it while kicking in a pair of three-inch heels.

I could tell a million more stories. There are more words and more memories, but nothing will ever take the place of being there and alive in the magical moments that were mine. Being backstage at Mötley Crüe and meeting Slash, the more than 150,000 kicks I performed as part of the Rockettes, standing in France on the side of the stage supporting Dreamer and looking out at the sea of people, knowing this was a once in a lifetime moment. I was there, I lived it. I made huge sacrifices for this life. Sometimes the world crashes down around me, and I wonder if it was all worth it. Other times I know it was.

One of the hardest things I ever had to learn in life is that the things that I love won't always love me back. It is heartbreaking. It is disappointing. But I have learned that this is just the way it is. Sometimes we have to get sad and cry and then the next day we have to put on our combat boots of life and stomp through the best we can. We can't get disappointed when the world doesn't give us what we gave it.

Following your dreams has little to do with talent. It has more to do with being a fighter, relentless in your dedication and focused. Someone once said that I should, "stop talking about hard work because I got handed everything on a silver platter." I wish that were true. I work hard and fight hard and really, only the last few years has really loved me back. I attended seven auditions in the last week, four in the last two days, along with dance classes, television classes and three rehearsal days. I book one out of every 20 jobs I audition for. I walk around feeling pretty terrible about myself most days. There are a hundred dancers better than me and a hundred worse.

But I love dancing. I love my place in the universe. I love this life even when it doesn't love me back. I moved to New York in a slow winter with $500 in my pocket. I made this life for myself, and I take full responsibility for all my successes and failures. As far as forgiveness goes, I've also learned that there is nothing more divine you can do than forgive someone who has wronged you.

As humanity evolves, we must take every day and every breath as if it's the first, last and only thing we have. If we constantly work on ourselves, our souls, and dealing with the influx of emotions, grudges, ego, hurt, happiness, forgiveness, resentment and mistakes, then we have only grown to deal with the past. If we see things and people in our lives as they were yesterday, then there has been no growth. We must give each other the constant ability to change. Everything that happened in the past never happened. I do not know that person or those days. I only know this day, this person standing before me and the words and actions as they say or do them in front of me. We must let everything and everyone in our lives evolve.

I've had amazing conversations with each of my rockstars and it really is true when they say time heals all wounds. It does. Things that seemed so important to me then are meaningless now. I said I would love my rockstars forever, and I meant it. I just love them in a different way. I'm thankful for the challenge of healing my heart after they left, because without them I would've never hit rockbottom and had to find my way out. On the way out of heartbreak, I found the most beautiful love ever, and after years of searching, crawling and confusion, I found the one true love of my life – myself.

On Feb. 16, 2009, I sat at my computer and started writing with my heavy broken heart. I was unable to take a shower because the act of being alone with only my thoughts was too scary.

On Feb. 17, I woke up with that same horrifically broken heart and was able to keep myself from crying for 42 minutes. I sat down at my computer and wrote down all the things I felt.

On Feb. 18, I decided to write a book. So I did.

Thank you...

My publisher Chris for believing in this story and for allowing me to do most of our meetings without pants on. To my editor Andriana Davis and very early editor Cristina Moreno for taking on the toughest job ever.

Spagatti, Boobs, CP, Nana, Kesh, Shu, Kristen and Carlos, Miss Loftiss, SA, She-She and Hobo – for being my best friends and for putting me back together when I was broken.

Jerry Mitchell, who should be too busy winning Tony Awards and directing shows for Broadway to write the most amazing foreword for little 'ol me, but wasn't.

My Rockette sisters for sharing all the things only someone who sits in a 40-degree ice bath with you on purpose can know about you. You were a part of my proudest moments. I love you.

To Steve and Challen and my entire my Sugar and Bruno Family, my dance teachers growing up who never gave up on me – Rebecca, Angie, Cyndi, Joanne, Sally and Shelley. Jacob Slitcher for your guidance and tea, and my most epic assistant ever, Kristina. Thank you.

To my Mom, Dad and Brother: I am well aware of all the sacrifices you all made so I could be the one in the family who got to have all her dreams come true. I feel so lucky to have such huge amounts of love and support from you. Thank you for giving me my wings and letting me jump into life so fearlessly. I was never scared, but I am sure you were. I love you.

My Highkicks and Highhopes Army: I started my blog because I loved dance and I loved love, and through that, I have come to love each and every one of you, dancers or not. Thank you for reading and being in my life. You mean more to me than words on paper could say. Courage. Passion. Hard Work.

And finally, thank you to Rocker, Singer and Dreamer for being incredible first loves.

Keltie Colleen is an established dancer and choreographer regularly featured in television and film. She is a former Radio City Rockette and New York Knicks dancer. Keltie blogs on life, love and dance at highkicksandhighhopes.blogspot.com. Keltie currently lives in Los Angeles with her dog, Hobo.